MW01634690

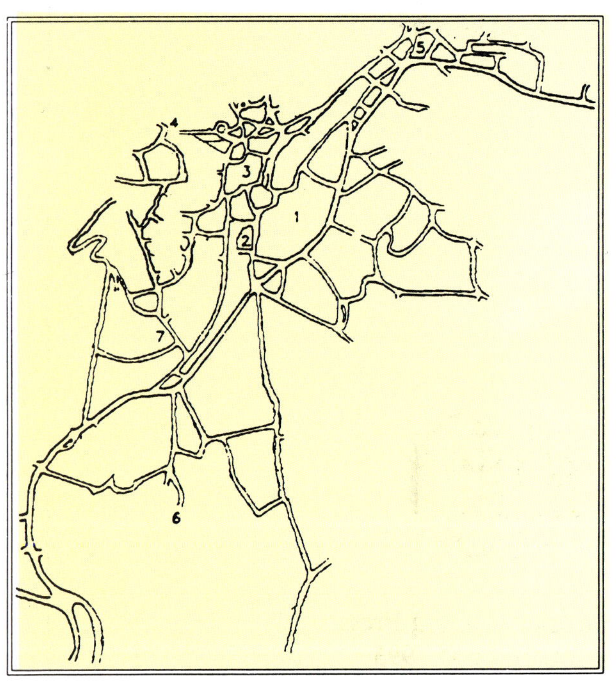

1: Basilica of the Annunciation, Friary of the Friars Minor and shrine of St. Joseph.
2: The Casa Nova.
3: Traditional site of the ancient Synagogue.
4: Mensa Christi.
5: The Virgin's Spring.
6: "Blessed Mother" of the Fright.
7: French Hospital.

HOLY PLACES OF PALESTINE

NAZARETH

Second Edition
Reprinted 1997

Franciscan Printing Press
JERUSALEM 1995

1. Paul VI visits Nazareth (January, 1964)
(Mosaic by Aldo Capri)

HOMILY OF POPE PAUL VI
During the Mass He celebrated at Nazareth

Nazareth is a kind of school where we may begin to discover what Christ's life was like and even to understand his Gospel. Here we can observe and ponder the simple appeal of the way God's Son came to be known, profound yet full of hidden meaning. And gradually we may even learn to imitate him.

Here we can learn to realize who Christ really is. And here we can sense and take account of the conditions and circumstances that surrounded and affected his life on earth: the places, the tenor of the times; the culture, the language, religious customs, in brief everything which Jesus used to make himself known to the world. Here everything speaks to us, everything has meaning. Here we can learn the importance of spiritual discipline for all who wish to follow Christ and to live by the teachings of His Gospel.

First we learn from its silence. If only we could once again appreciate its great value. We need this wonderful state of mind, beset as we are by the cacophony of strident protests and conflicting claims so characteristic of these turbulent times. The silence of Nazareth should teach us how to meditate in peace and quiet, to reflect on the deeply spiritual, and to be open to the voice of God's inner wisdom and the counsel of his true teachers. Nazareth can teach us the value of study and preparation, of meditation, of a well-ordered personal spiritual life, and of silent prayer that is known only to God.

Second we learn about family life. May Nazareth serve as a model of what the family should be. May it show us the family's holy and enduring character and exemplifying its basic function in society: a community of love and sharing, beautiful for the problems it poses and the rewards it brings; in sum, the perfect setting for rearing children — and for this there is no substitute.

Finally, in Nazareth, the home of a craftsman's son, we learn about work and the discipline it entails. I would especially like to recognize its value — demanding yet redeeming — and to give it proper respect. I would remind everyone that work has its own dignity. On the other hand, it is not an end in itself. Its value and free character, however, derive not only from its place in the economic system, as they say, but rather from the purpose it serves.

In closing, may I express my deep regard for people everywhere who work for a living. To them I would point out their great model, Christ their brother, our Lord and God, who is their prophet in every cause that promotes their well being.

I

NAZARETH IN GALILEE

The word "Galilee", *Galila* in the Greek papyrus of Zenon (Third Century B.C.), is borrowed from the Hebrew word *galil* which means *"district"*. The Bible mentions it as Galilee of the Nations (Is. 9,23), as the Land of Galilee (I Kings 9,11), or simply as Galilee (Joshua 20,7). These expressions presuppose a distinction between Jewish Galilee in a strict sense and the territory which was inhabited mostly by non-Jews. Flavius Josephus is the first one to distinguish between Upper and Lower Galilee. This terminology has come into modern use and now is accepted by modern geographers. The differences of height, climate and vegetation give the term validity. The peaks in Upper Galilee rise above 3,000 feet, but in Lower Galilee they are under 1,800 feet. As far as Flavius Josephus, the first century historian, was concerned, Galilee included Phoenicia and Syria. It was bounded on the west by

2. View of Nazareth from the surrounding heights.

Akko-Ptolomais and Mt Carmel; on the south by Samaria and Bethshean; on the east by the lands of the cities of Hippos and Gadara and the Golan; and on the north by the land of Tyre or Phoenicia (Jewish Wars III, 3). The natural division between Upper and Lower Galilee is the valley of Betha Kerem and the ravine of Wadi Amud.

Geographically the mountains of Upper Galilee are part of the elevated plain which extends northward as far as the valley of the Litani river, which today is separated politically by the border between Lebanon and Israel. The mean height is 1,970 ft. with peaks as high as 3,135 ft. in Jebel Canaan north of Safed, and 3,965 ft. in Jebel Jarmak or Har Meron. The terrain in that area is rough with large forests and has had a fairly sparse population both in ancient and modern times. On its eastern side the Galilean plateau overlooks the plain of Huleh with a drop of 1,300 to 2,300 ft. On this side, in a basin, the city of Kadesh flourished which was the most important city center in the mountainous territory which the tribe of Nephtali occupied.

Lower Galilee has the plain of Esdraelon on the south, the basin with the Sea of Galilee on the east and the hilly uplands with their valleys in the north beginning with the hills of Nazareth (1,880 ft.). Single heights like Mt. Tabor (1,930 ft.) and Mt. Moreh or Jebel Jahi (1,690 ft.) begin to rise on the eastern edge of the Plain of Esdraelon (165 ft.) to the edge of the basalt plateau of Issachar which looks out over the Sea of Galilee and the valley of Jordan from a height of 2,300 ft. During the Greek-Roman period the capital changed back and forth between Sepphoris and Tiberias. Today Nazareth is the political and administrative center of Galilee.

David Roberts R.A.

II

THE LITERARY SOURCES

The city, today the political and administrative capital of Galilee, first appears in the story found in the pages of the Gospel. *"The Angel Gabriel was sent by God to a city of Galilee named Nazareth, to a virgin betrothed to a man with the name Joseph of the house of David. The name of the virgin was Mary"*(Lk 1, 26-27). In compliance with the *"decree of Caesar Augustus which called for a census of the whole empire... Joseph too went from Galilee, from the city of Nazareth, to Judea, to the city of David which is called Bethlehem... to get registered with Mary his spouse who was with child."*(Lk 2, 1-4). Upon his return from Egypt where he had fled with Mary and the Child Jesus, Joseph *"returned to the land of Galilee and settled in a town called Nazareth."* Luke twice repeats, after the presentation of Jesus in the Temple (Lk 2,39) and after the journey of the Holy Family to Jerusalem: *"(Jesus) went up with them*

3. Nazareth in 1838 (lithograph of D. Roberts).

THE ANNUNCIATION

In the sixth month, the angel Gabriel was sent by God to a city of Galilee, called Nazareth, to a virgin espoused to a man of the house of David called Joseph. The virgin was called Mary. He entered and said: "Greetings to you, full of grace, the Lord is with you". She was troubled at these words and inquired about the meaning of such a greeting. The angel said to her: "Do not fear, Mary, since you have found grace before God. Behold you will concieve a son, give birth to him and you will call him Jesus. He will be great and called Son of the Most High; the Lord God will give to him the throne of David and he will rule forever over the house of Jacob and there will be no end to his reign".

Then Mary said to the angel: "How can this be possible? I do not know man". The angel answered her "The Holy Spirit will come down upon you, He will spread upon you the shadow of the power of the Most High. The one born will therefore be holy and will be called Son of God. Look: Elizabeth, too, your relative, in her advanced years, has conceived a son and this is her sixth month, and they were considering her as sterile: nothing is impossible for God". And so Mary Said: "Behold me! I am the servant of the Lord, let what you have said happen to me". Then the angel left her.

(Luke 1,26-38)

JESUS AT NAZARETH

Jesus returned in the power of the Spirit to Galilee, and his reputation spread throughout the region. He was teaching in their synagogues, and all were loud in his praise.

He came to Nazareth where he had been reared, and entering the synagogue on the sabbath as he was in the habit of doing, he stood up to do the reading. When the book of the prophet Isaiah was handed him, he unrolled the scroll and found the passage where it was written:

"The spirit of the Lord is upon me; therefore, he has anointed me. He has

sent me to bring glad tidings to the poor, to proclaim liberty to captives, Recovery of sight to the blind and release to prisoners To announce a year of favor from the Lord."

Rolling up the scroll he gave it back to the assistant and sat down. All in the synagogue had their eyes fixed on him. Then he began by saying to them, "Today this scripture passage is fulfilled in your hearing." All who were present spoke favorably of him; they marveled at the appealing discourse which came from his lips. They also asked, "Is not this Joseph's son?"

He said to them, "You will doubtless quote me the proverb, 'Physician heal yourself,' and say, 'Do here in your own country the things we have heard you have done in Capernaum.' But in fact", he went on, "no prophet gains acceptance in his native place. Indeed, let me remind you, there were many widows in Israel in the days of Elijah when the heavens remained closed for three and a half years and a great famine spread over the land. It was to none of these that Elijah was sent, but to a widow of Zarephath near Sidon. Recall, too, the many lepers in Israel in the time of Elisha the prophet; yet not one was cured except Naaman the Syrian."

At these words the whole audience in the synagogue was filled with indignation. They rose up and expelled him from the town leading him to the brow of the hill on which it was built and intending to hurl him over the edge. But he went straight through their midst and walked away.

(Luke 4, 14-30)

4. Clay memento of the Annunciation (VI century).

and returned to Nazareth, and was subject to them. And his mother kept all these things in her heart. Then Jesus grew in wisdom, size and grace before God and men"(Lk 2, 51ff). The information from Matthew helps explain the name "Nazarean" given to Jesus (Mt. 2,23).

Early in his ministry as a travelling rabbi, Jesus left Nazareth and went down to Capharnaum on the bank of the lake (Mt 4,13). As he preached the Kingdom in the villages of the Galilean hinter land he was led back again to Nazareth. There in the synagogue he presented his fellow citizens with a commentary on the passage of Isaia which was fulfilled in his person: *"And he came to Nazareth where he had been raised. On a Sabbath, as was his custom, he went into the synagogue and he stood up to read... they rose up and drove him out of the city. They led him to the edge of a hill on which their city was build, to throw him down"* (Lk 4, 16-30; Mt 13, 54-58; Mk 6, 1-6). This rejection by his own neighbors is expressed in a lively way when Matthew and Mark describe the event: *He reached his own land and taught them in their synagogue in such a way that they were surprised and said: "Where does this wisdom and these miracles come from? Is not he the son of the carpenter? Is not his mother called Mary, and his brothers James, Joseph, Simon and Jude? And are not his sisters all among us?..."* (Mt 13, 54-58; Mk 6, 1-6).

His Nazareth origin is why Nathaniel at first rejected Him. When Jesus was introduced to him his cynical answer was: *"Can anything good come from Nazareth?"* (Jn 1,46). Nevertheless, the village from which he came became forever linked to the name of Jesus. *"And Jesus of Nazareth"* is the one who was welcomed in the villages (Mk 10,46 ff). *"It was Jesus the Nazarene"* that the band of soldiers was looking for in the garden of Gethsemane (Jn 18,5). It was as *"Jesus the Nazarene, the king of the Jews"* that he was condemned to death on the cross by Pilate (Jn 19,19). It was Jesus of Nazareth whom Peter and the Apostles preached that rose on the third day (Acts 10,38 ff). The Jewish sources knew him as *Jesus the Nazarene* (Jesu ha-Nosri) and call his followers the *Nazarenes* (ha-Nosrim).

Among the first followers and the ones who carried out the work of Jesus, the sources mention "the brothers of the Lord" (Acts 1,14; 1 Cor 9,5). Because of their bond of kinship they would most probably have responsible positions and enjoy much respect in the primitive Palestinian church. James directed the church of Jerusalem as both the Acts (21,8) and Flavius Josephus (AJ XX, 197-203) record. Simeon, "cousin of the Lord" succeeded him and was martyred during the time of Trajan.

The Judeo-Christian historian, Heggesippus (second half of the II century) mentions some relatives of Jesus, nephews of Jude, on the occasion

5. The Annunciation and the Visitation.
(Armenian Lectionary from 1014)

of a persecution during the time of the emperor Domitian (81-96 A.D.). The text is quoted by the historian Eusebius (4th century) in his Historia Ecclesiastica III, 19.20, 1-6:

An ancient tradition mentions that when this Domitian ordered the suppression of the descendants of David, some heretics took the occasion to denounce also the descendants of Jude who was the blood brother of the Saviour, as belonging to the descendants of David and the family of Jesus. Heggesippus reports this information in these words: Of the family of the Lord there still remain the nephews of Jude, said to be his blood brother. They were denounced as being among the descendants of David. The soldier brought them before Caesar Domitian because he also, like Herod, feared the coming of Christ. And he asked them if they descended from David and they confirmed the fact. Then he asked them how much property and how much money they had. They answered that they had in all nine thousand denarii, a half for each one of them, and they said that they did not have it in ready cash. But that it was the value of a piece of land of only thirty nine plethrum. They had paid the tax on it, they lived on the land and cultivated it themselves. And they showed him their hands as testimony of their pesonal work causing the roughness of their body and the callouses on their hands, caused by their constant toil. They were interrogated about Christ and His reign, His nature and the time and place when he would appear. They answered that his reign was not of this world nor of this land, but it was heavenly and angelic and it would be fulfilled at the end of the centuries, when Christ would come in His glory and judge the living and the dead and render to each person according to their own works. Then Domitian did not condemn them at all, but he scorned them as being persons of little importance. He let them go and through an edict he brought an end to the persecution against the church. Once they were freed they became leaders in the churches because they were both witnesses and relatives of the Lord. When peace was restored they remained alive until the time of Trajan.

This event emphasizes the social situation of the family members of Jesus. They were peasants who lived by hard daily work, and they had a special position in the church. Julius Africanus (ca 250) notes that the relatives of Jesus *"from the Jewish villages of Nazareth and Kokaba were scattered about in various regions"* jealously kept the family records (passage is contained in Eusebius, St. Eccl. 1,7,13-14). During the persecution of Decius (249-251 A.D.), in Asia Minor Conon was taken to trial because he was a Christian. This martyr declared in court: *"I am from the city of Nazareth in Galilee. I am among the relatives of Christ to whom I have been offering homage since the days of my forefathers."*

Christian apocryphal literature offers other details about the family of Jesus drawn from Christian tradition. *The Proto-Evangelium of James mentions Joachim and Anna as the parents of Mary. The History of Joseph the carpenter* speaks about the end of Joseph, his death and burial at Nazareth. This anonymous author describes Jesus at the bedside of his dying father as he says: *"The time for my father to die arrived just as it does for all humans. I went into the room of the fine elderly man and greeted him with affection and a word of encouragement. My visit made him happy and he brightened up. Then I sat down at his feet and I looked at him... I held his hands for an hour: and he turned his face toward me and did not want me to leave him... In that way he passed away calmly... Together with Mary my mother and our relatives we wept for that nice elderly gentleman.. It was I who closed his eyes.."*

As far as monuments are concerned, the first person to write about buildings for Christian religious services which developed in Nazareth was Epiphanius. He mentions the attempt of count Joseph of Tiberias, a Jewish convert at the time of Constantine, to erect a church in the village. A Jewish source, the *Elegy of Eleazar ha Kalir,* mentions a priestly family, *Ha Pizzez,* whose name had been inserted into the list of service shifts for the temple on the Sabbath day (shifts called *mishmarot*), who lived at Nazareth. This is confirmed by a Hebrew inscription found at Cae-

6. Seal of Robert, bishop of Nazareth during the Crusader period.

sarea which lists the varous *mishmarot*. In this inscription, the name of Nazareth is legible. Eusebius, in his *Onomasticon,* mentions the geographical position of the village: *"Nazareth, which is why Jesus was called Nazarene, and why we ourselves were once called Nazarenes but now Christians, still today is in Galilee 15 miles eastward from the lake, near Mount Tabor".*

Paola and Eustochio, accompanied by Jerome, came on pilgrimage "with quick steps" and it was he who called the little village of Nazareth *"the flower of Galilee".* The Anonymous Pilgrim of Piacenza (570) wrote that in Nazareth he had seen "many marvelous things" and visited the synagogue with its memories of the infancy of Jesus. He added: *"The house of holy Mary is now a basilica and many are the blessings that come to anyone who succeeds in touching her clothing. The number of Hebrew women who come there is very large. And in that land are found the most beautiful of women. They say that this grace has been given to them by holy Mary, and they even claim that she is their ancestor".*

The Patriarch of Alexandria Eutichus tells us that when the Emperor Heraclius, who had been victorious over the Persians (629) arrived, the Jews of Nazareth came to meet him and asked for his protection. At first he granted their request, but later on he withdrew it because of the pressure of the Christians in Jerusalem who requested the Emperor to vindicate the outrages the Jews inflicted on them during the Persian occupation (XV, 1-6).

During the Arab occupation after 638, Arculf came as a pilgrim. He told

Abbot Adamanno that he saw two churches in Nazareth: *one in which our Saviour was nourished,* the other, the Church of the Annunciation. When Willibaldo came in 724-26 only the church of the Annunciation was still to be seen. The same was mentioned again by the Arab traveller Al Mas'udi.

In the midst of the abandoned houses of the village, the victorious Crusaders very quickly began to reconstruct the shrine, as is narrated by Saewulf, the English pilgrim who came in 1102: *The city of Nazareth was completely devastated and shattered by the Saracens, but at the place of the Annunciation of the Lord there was a very fine monastery".* Because of the importance of this shrine, Nazareth became an episcopal see. The Norman Tancred to whom the principality of Galilee had been given, made it his duty to adorn the restored Basilica sumptuously with gifts of every sort. This was mentioned by William of Tyre, the historian contemporary to the Crusades as well as in the descriptions of those pilgrims who were able to visit the shrine in all its splendor: the Russian Abbot Daniel, Theodoric and John Focas.

On the very same day as the disastrous battle of Hattin, July 4, 1187, Nazareth too was taken and what was left of the population was taken prisoner. One witness said: *"Other Saracens went up into the city of Nazareth and stained the church with blood, slaughtering the Christians who fled there on account of its fortifications; I am speaking about the holy church known in the whole world and adorned by the faithful in honor of the Word Incarnate... After they destroyed the city and profaned the sacred Places they took the road across a certain brow of the mountain called "The Lord's Leap" and went on to Tabor"*(Raul di Coggeshall). In the following period, thanks to the peace treaties, the shrine could be used and visited even though in a reduced form. On March 24, 1251 St. Louis IX, king of France participated in the Mass celebrated by his chaplain in the Grotto of the Annunciation. In 1263 the basilica was systematically destroyed by order of the sultan Bibars. The historian Abu el-Feda, in his annals wrote: *"During a pause on Mt. Tabor, a detachment of his army went to Nazareth by his order and destroyed the church of this city".*

The few pilgrims who ventured East after the fall of the Latin Kingdom refer to a poor village in which Moslems lived and a few communities of eastern monks. In 1243 a document from the Venetian archives makes mention of a hospital which some holy women operated for the assistance of pilgrims. The Franciscans who had been coming in

7. Mazreth around 1865.

pilgrimage to the shrine took possession of the Crusader basilica and the Grotto in 1620. Another date to keep in mind is 1730, the year in which the Franciscans were able to erect a church over the holy grotto.

III

NAZARETH

Literary sources show that Nazareth has been inhabited from the first century until today. But archaeology examines what is underground. From both planned excavations and some accidental discoveries we know that the ancient village was located in the area of the modern city. And it has been in existence there since 2,000 B.C. Between 1890 and 1910 Father Prospero Viaud and Fra Benedetto Vlamink began excavations in the area of the Franciscan Friary. They were continued by Father Bellarmino Bagatti during the years of 1955-1970. In 1884 underground excavations at the convent of the Dames de Nazaret were begun and taken up again in 1940. Accidental discoveries include a few tombs from scattered times and an inscription in Greek. This is now in Paris in the Gabinetto delle Medaglie, sent there from Nazareth in 1878. On the marble slab is written a decree of Caesar Augustus which makes the desecration of Tombs a sacrilege punishable by death.

8. St. John the Baptist. Sketched on the plaster of the Judeo-Christian synagogue near the Grotto of the Anunciation.

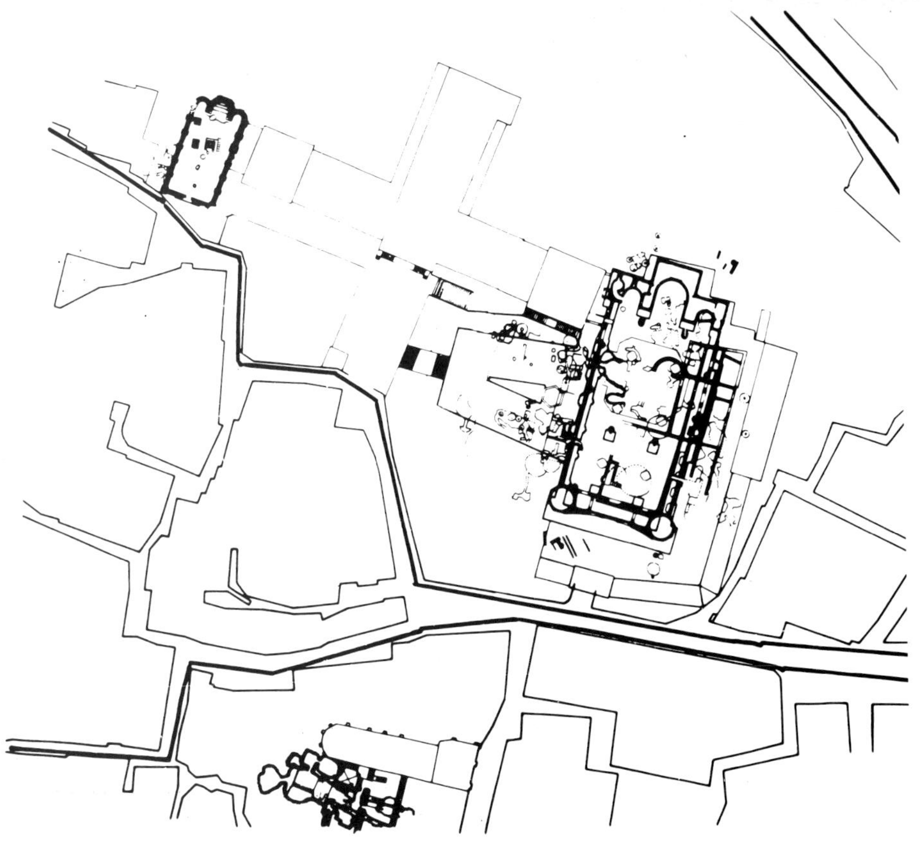

9. Main areas of the excavations at Nazareth: Basilica of the Annunciation, church of St. Joseph, excavations at the Dames de Nazaret (at bottom).

Remains of the village

Luke, the evangelist, writes that Nazareth was situated on a hillside (Lk 4,29). Excavations lead us to conclude that the ancient village was located on the hill in the center of the modern city. Tombs were found to the south of the Basilica of the Annunciation and to the west on the depression of the amphi-theater-shaped hill where the modern city is spread out. This more or less marks off the dwellings discovered in the area of the Franciscan Friary between the Basilica and the church of St. Joseph, and westward as far as the Greek Catholic church.

10. Ceramic patterns from the Iron Age found in a Nazareth tomb. (10th century B.C.).

11. Ceramic patterns from the Roman Period found at Nazareth. (First century A.D.)

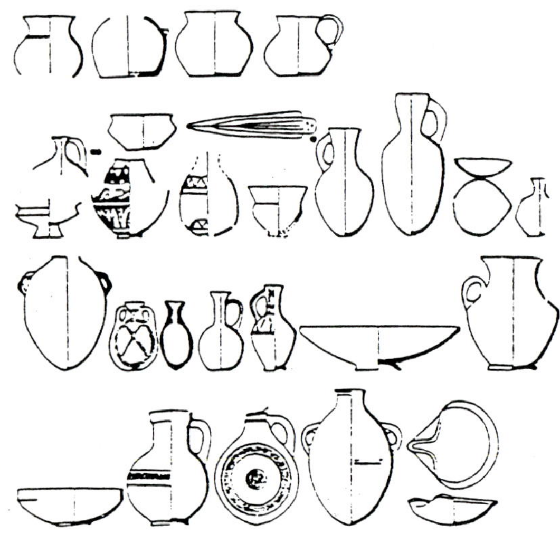

12-13. A bronze dagger with ceramic patterns from Middle Bronze and the Iron Age found at Nazareth (XX-X century B.C.)

The largest section of the village which has been excavated until now is located in the basement of the Basilica of the Annunciation and on the other side of its northern wall. There Fr. Bagatti was able to trace a continuous human presence from the first centuries of the Second millenium B.C. until the present.

The Shrine of the Annunciation

Where today there is the Basilica of the Annunciation, consecrated in the spring of 1969, there was until the 1950's a small, simple church which the Franciscans build in 1730 over the grotto which the Christians of Nazareth venerated as the Grotto of the Annunciation.

In 1890 Father Prospero Viaud, Guardian of the convent took an interest in the archaeological and historical questions of the place and began to remove the walls of the convent. He noted that these walls were partially built on the north wall of the Crusader basilica. He worked methodically and brought to light the whole basilica (246 ft x 98 ft) upon whose foundations the present basilica is built. Within it he found sections of the mosaic floor of the church of the Byzantine period.

When the Custody of the Holy Land made the decision to tear down the church of 1730 and put in its place a more dignified structure the way was opened for the second phase of the exploration of the area. This excavation was done by Fr. Bellarmine Bagatti of the Studium Biblicum Franciscanum during the years 1955-1962. The first result was the determination of the plan of the Byzantine church to which belonged the mosaics discovered by Fr. Viaud. The church was rather small, with three naves and an atrium on the west with a small convent on the south. At the same time it became clear that the holy Grotto was situated within the more southern part of the village. This put a final end to scholarly arguments regarding the authenticity of the shrine. There had been some scholars who cast doubt on the Grotto, contending that it was the result of local piety without historical basis because it stood on a necropolis, a location incompatible with the Jewish rules of legal purity.

14. Father Bellarmine Bagatti (1905-1992) who directed the modern excavations of Nazareth.

15. Capital of the Shrine with a cross dating from the Byzantine period.

When the mosaics were taken up so that the excavation could probe deeper, the greatest surprise came. The fill underneath was made up of bases of columns, shells, rubble and colored plaster. All of it came from the time when an earlier synagogue building was torn down. By reading and interpreting the graffiti which had been scratched on the plaster or traced with carbon, it became clear that it had been a place of cult, and it had been a shrine used by Christians. The graffiti were certainly more ancient than the mosaics which covered them. They come from the 4th century, or even the first decades of the 5th century. They are clearly legible invocations to the Virgin Mary, in Greek.

Historically, the data to pay attention to is the building itself. But also to be considered, is the fact that there had been veneration, by christian pilgrims, for that place made holy by the presence of Mary, and in the village of her origin.

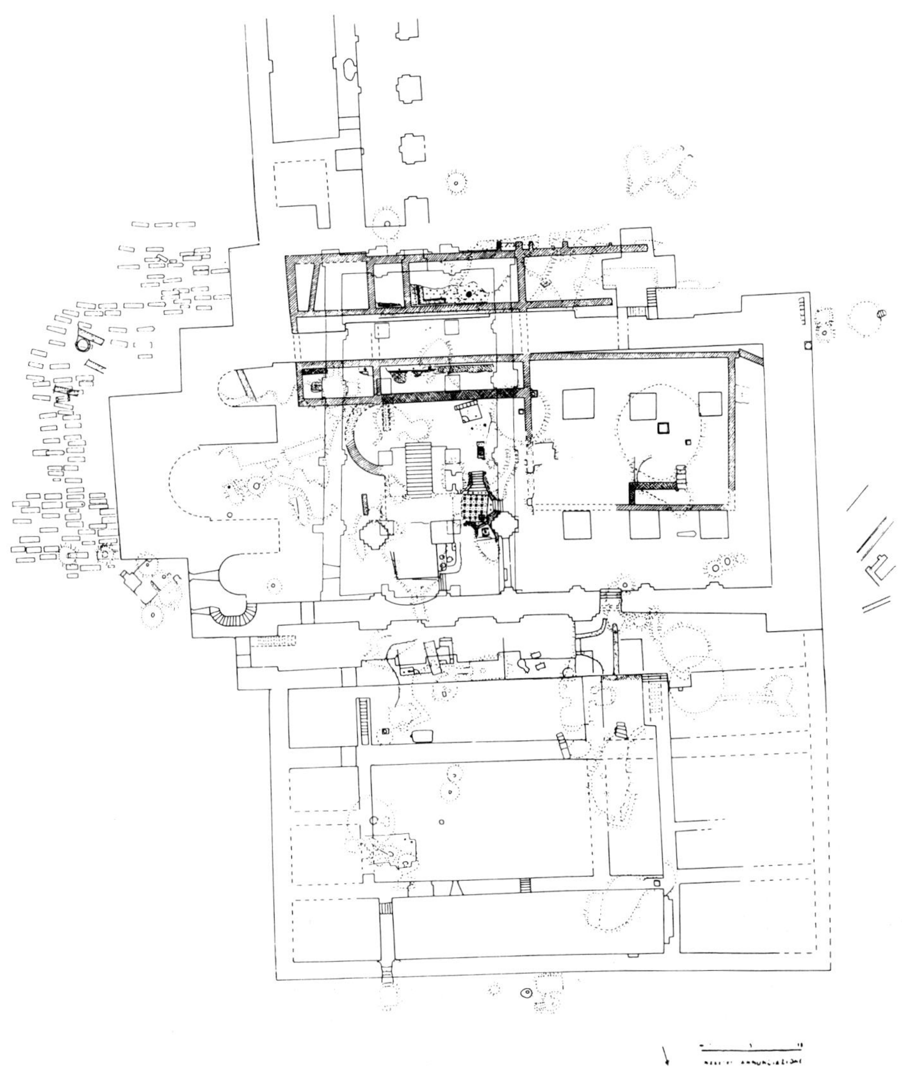

16. Plan of the Antiquities in the ancient village of Nazareth in the property of the Custody of the Holy Land. They date from the Roman era to the construction of the Crusader Basilica of the Annunciation. (12th entury A.D.).

17. A golden ring with the Annunciation scene. (Sixth century)

We focus our attention on a synagogue, a place of cult, therefore, used by Jewish Christians, who were descendents of the Nazarenes. After they overcame their first mistrust, they came to believe in Jesus, their fellow citizen. Among these people are to be numbered those same relatives of Jesus about which the Gospels and ancient sources speak.

The Church of St. Joseph

Fr. Quaresmi, around 1620, had already refered to the apses of the Crusader church. In 1754 the Franciscans took possession of the apse area. They changed it into a chapel. In 1858 they built a small church.

18. Sketch of the excavations by Fr. Prospero Viaud in the area of the Church of St. Joseph with some remains of the Crusader apses.

At that time a section of mosaic flooring was discovered. In 1890 they acquired the whole area of the church and excavations gave Fr. Viaud the opportunity to uncover the complete plan of the Crusader church. In the underground limestone appeared a cistern and a basin with steps leading to a mosaic floor at the bottom. There was also a set of silos in which one was carved on top of the other. Along the side of the cistern, was a corridor carved in the rock with the top holes of the silos used for ventilation. In 1970, in a trench outside the northern wall of the church, Fr. Bagatti found other underground passages and other silos carved in the rock. There were also ceramic pieces which date from the Iron Age (eighth century B.C.) down to our own day.

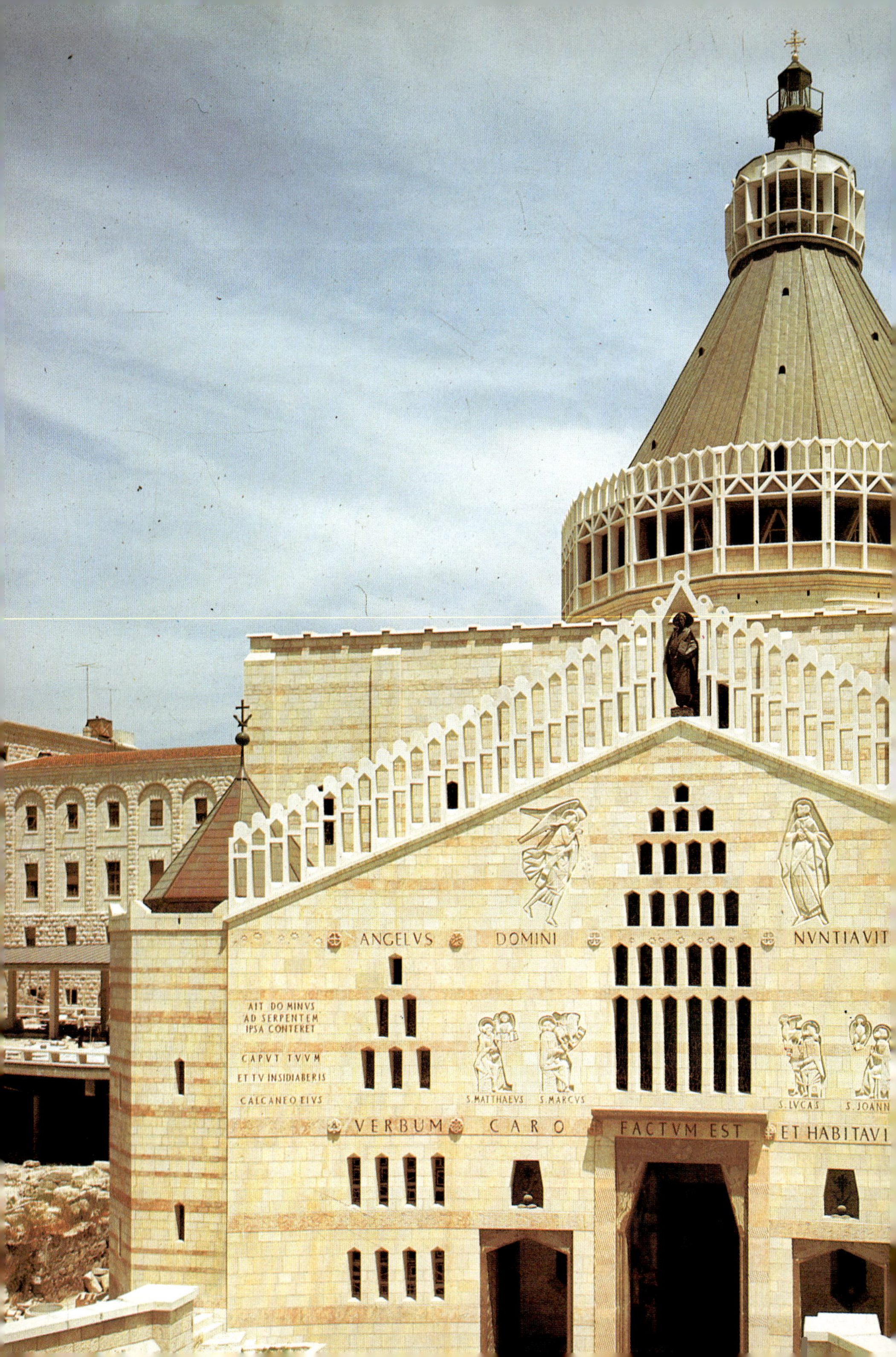
ANGELVS DOMINI NVNTIAVIT
AIT DOMINVS
AD SERPENTEM
IPSA CONTERET
CAPVT TVVM
ET TV INSIDIABERIS
CALCANEO EIVS
S. MATTHAEVS
S. MARCVS
S. LVCAS
S. JOANN
VERBVM CARO FACTVM EST ET HABITAVI

IV

THE BASILICA OF THE ANNUNCIATION

Public admittance to the Shrine is made through the west entrance way. A porch there is the cloister for the Basilica. On the left are some layers protruding from the facade of the Crusader basilica. The facade of today, slightly concave and set in between two towers, highlights the mystery of the Incarnation. Above in the top front center is Christ the Redemmer (bronze by Angelo Biancini, 10ft. high), the God-Man, firstborn of all creatures. At the appropriate time for his plan for the redemption of humanity to unfold, God the Father sent Him upon the earth, born of a woman, in order to usher in atonement through the blood of His cross. It was in the womb of Mary of Nazareth, at the instant of the Annunciation, that the Word was made flesh and dwelt among us. This theme is developed in the bas-relief of the facade designed by Biancini and engraved in

19. The basilica of the Annunciation (Architect: John Muzio) consecrated in 1969.

the stone of the facade by Mr. Cornelio Turelli. Four decorative bands symbolically recall our universe in which God through Jesus wanted to take part: Land, Sea, Heaven, and the flaming Heaven, abode of the angels, according to Judeo-Christian cosmography (design of A. Maiocchi executed by the stonecutter Najib Noufi). Above the architrave are the four Evangelists, authentic witnesses of the life of Jesus among us.

The three bronze doors (made by Roland Friederichsen) once more take up these themes and elaborate upon them. The two side doors in embossed copper have a trapezoidal band attached which emphasizes the texts of Scripture which explain the reliefs of the door and develop the messanic prophecies of the Old Testament. The door on the left depicts those texts from Creation to the sacrifice of Isaac. On the right are those from David to Jonah. The central doorway in two sides (13 ft high x 10 ft wide), is designed with six framed panels and a written text as an explanation. It has a portal frame of rose colored marble on which is carved the Trinity, the source of the plan of salvation which already had been foretold many times and in various ways to the Fathers through means of the Prophets (sculpturer is Turelli according to the designs of Maiocchi). Fathers revered on the left door jamb are: Adam planting the tree of life from which, in the distant future, would be cut the wood of the Cross, according to a Judeo-christian

20. The Annunciation and the four Evangelists (detail of the facade).

21. The bronze and copper door with the History of Salvation (Roland Friederichsen).

myth. The plan of salvation announced to the world by the Apostles is recorded on the right door jamb.

On the door, the life of Jesus is represented in 16 episodes: 6 scenes are in cast bronze altorelief, and around them are 10 scenes in copper relief. The left double door is devoted to the infancy of Jesus, beginning from above: Birth, Flight into Egypt, life in Nazareth. The double door on the right side represents the public life of the Lord Jesus, from the bottom to top: Baptism, Beatitudes, Crucifixion.

There is a second lesser facade straight across from the holy grotto on the south wall of the Basilica. It is dedicated to the Virgin Mary. The words of the Salve Regina are engraved on the outside wall and in the center is a statue of Mary of Nazareth (bronze by F. Verroca). There is a balcony protruding from the wall above the door for imparting blessings. On the inside of the little atrium adorned with a mosaic by Prof. Salvoni, is the place where the doors open. The central bronze door, the work of the American F. Shrady, tells the story of the Blesed Mother. The two side doors in embossed copper (work of Genni Mucchi) express the themes of the Litany of Loretto.

Around the court yard there is a portico. On its walls are representations of the more outstanding shrines of the nations which provided the scenes. A lodge is located there with an impressive overlook upon the valley below.

22. The bronze doors with the scene of the life of Mary of Nazareth. (F. Shrady).

23. The south facade with the statue of the Virgin Mary and the text of the "Hail Holy Queen." (V. Verroca).

The Grotto of the Annunciation

For many centuries the Grotto of the Annunciation has been the focal point of devotion for Christians coming from a great difference of origin and mentality. They brought with them endless changes needed for their services. First an altar was erected to the east and later in the center of the grotto. The ceiling was raised, adjusted and punctured, the floor was lowered, the walls were patched with masonry. Despite all this there is still something left of the original arrangement of the place as part of a family dwelling.

The main elements of this history are in the drawing (fig. 26), of the inside of the Holy Grotto. Viewed from bottom to top.

1. A round hollow area in the rock. It can be seen above from the wrought iron railing outside the grotto. It is the remains of an early dwelling which was in use before the cultic changes were made. It is a "silo" cut in the rock in

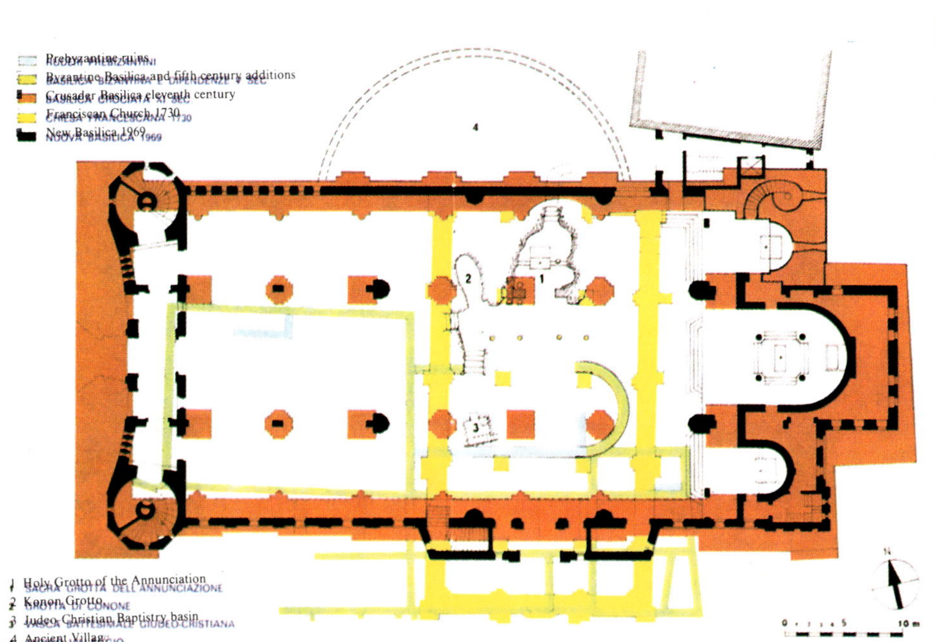

24. The Grotto of the Annunciation after the recent restoration. In the center is the altar of the Franciscan church built in 1730.

25. The plan of the Basilica of the Annunciation with the Holy Grotto.

which various kinds of cereals could be stored. The bottom part of the silo is preserved ın tact under the floor. The opening, 31 inches above the "chapel of th angel", shows the level of the rock floor of the room.

2. A second silo similar to the first.

3. Inside the grotto, to the left, are five courses of good ancient bricks. They are much like those at the entrance of the nearby small alcove with the mosaics and pictures. When the first memorial was being built a need was felt to remake one of the walls of the grotto.

4. The ceiling of the inside of the Grotto is round in shape, like the dome of a small church. In the course of time, holes and vents became necessary to let in fresh air and to extract the smoke of the lamps.

5. There is a small apse carved into the rock on the east side. From the Byzantine times until 1730 there was an altar there. The apse was plastered over many times. Up to five layers of plaster have been counted.

6. In the upper part of the apse is an unsightly hole made by the Crusaders when they rested the foundations of a pillar too near the wall of the Grotto. Unfortunately the damage is increasing because the rock itself is so fragile.

7. Outside the Grotto the Crusader builders placed three large granite columns as a foundation for another pillar. Thus the maximum amount of space was made available for the Grotto. Now two columns are still there outside the Grotto. The larger one was called "*Column of the Angel*" and the opening between the two columns is called the "*Window of the Angel*".

8. The third column protruded above the ceiling of the Grotto. The Crusaders patched the ceiling and the column remained isolated in this corner of the room. Pilgrims call it the "*Column of the Virgin*". The lower part of the column was smashed by someone looking for treasure.

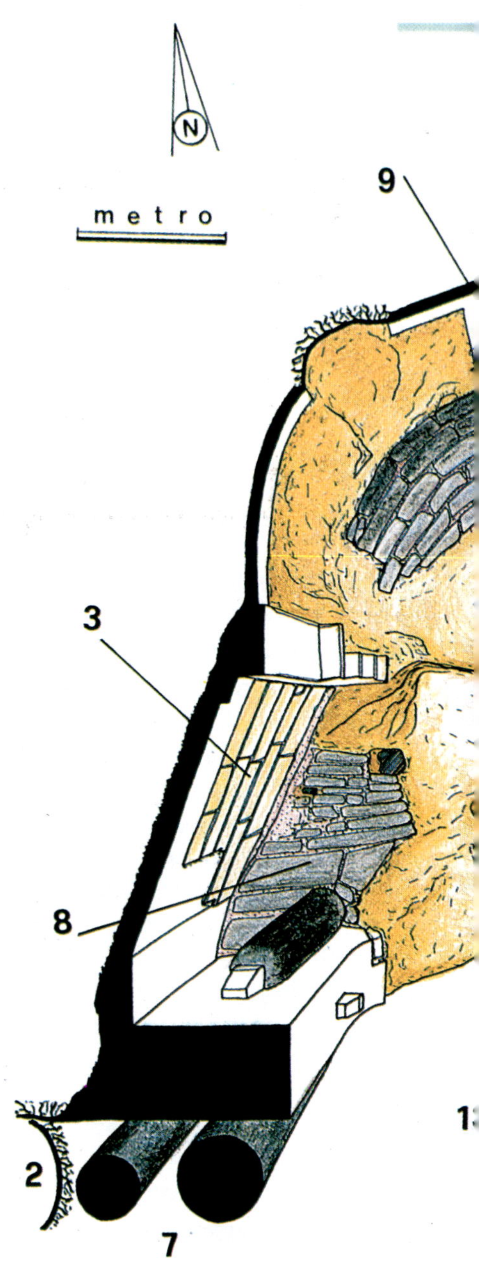

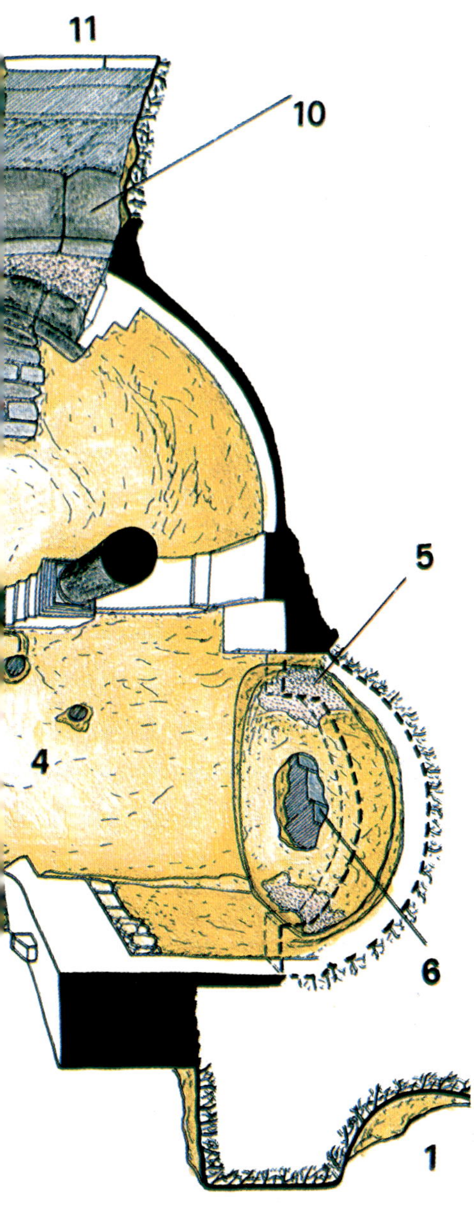

26. A persepctive drawing of the walls and ceiling of the Grotto of the Annunciation.

9. The interior section of the Grotto is semicircular in shape. It too is ancient, although not in its present form. Part of the dome was remade in masonry during the days of the Crusaders.

10. Two large curved stones are part of the foundation of the north wall of the Crusader apse.

11. In the 17th century the Franciscans carved out this underground passageway to have direct access from the convent to the Holy Grotto. Even in ancient times there was a tunnel to connect up with other grottos more to the north which was part of a press for wine.

12. The square frame, easily seen up above, is the remains of a marble plaque on which was a valuable painting of the Spanish school. It was placed above the altar in 1730. The mensa is still used today for the Eucharist.

V

THE LOWER BASILICA

The new basilica, externally a single block of reinforced concrete decorated with stones quarried locally, on the inside is composed of two enormous halls, one above the other. Between the two is an "oculus" opening with the cupola rising above it in the shape of an inverted lily. Two helical staircases in the front facade and a third staircase along the southern facade lead up and down between the two churches.

The lower church is dimly lighted with its soft light coming from the colored glass windows (work of Lidia Roppolt). It should be noted how the north walls rest on the foundation walls of the Crusader basilica uncovered during the new construction to a height of 10 to 13 feet with the half-columns and original rows of stone for its whole length. The reinforced concrete beams of the nave duplicate the square or bundled pillars of the Crusader basilica.

At the height of the third pillar two of the four pylons rise up. They support the cupola and the floor of the upper

27. Eucharistic celebration in front of the Grotto of the Annunciation.

28. Detail of the north wall of the Basilica of the Crusader period (12th century).

church. They also make possible the large open area in the center of the basilica which allows for the full effect of the view of the grotto and the other elements of antiquity discovered in the archaeological excavation. It is all bordered by the iron bannister. The Grotto, for the most part natural, is carved out along the side of the apse which the crusader architect made. On the north wall are remains of sacred buildings that were formely on, or underneath it.

In order not to disturb the shape of the vault in respect to a pillar that hung from the ceiling, the Crusader architect made it rest on two granite columns which jet out from inside the grotto. The Byzantine people made their church match the uneven level of the hill which at this point is very irregular. Thus they made good use of its abnormal shape, just like the inhabitants of the place did in their dwellings.

The modern architects designed the four pillars which support the cupola in the center of the building. It has been done in such a way as to leave the sacred space free and uncluttered and let it be illumined solely by the light falling from above.

Externally the Grotto looks like an isolated rocky cubicule surrounded by the adjoining apse on the northern wall of the basilica. Internally it is like a stone chapel in the shape of a roundish apse on its east (18 ft from north to

29. Greek inscription of the deacon Conon of Jerusalem.

south, 20.1 ft from west to east, 9.8 ft in height). The remains of silos on the floor level and fragments of ceramics in the cracks of the roof show that there is no difference there and the underground of the living quarters of the village discovered nearby. But the changes made in the area for religious services have made it impossible for us today to picture what the original house of the Virgin was like. An examination of the plaster applied to the walls of the little grotto on the western side supplies historical evidence sufficient to say when this change had already taken place. The little grotto is called the *"Grotto of Conon"*, according to the name of the deacon from Jerusalem who had the floor mosaic put in, as is mentioned at the entrance. The little grotto today looks like a room positioned toward the north west with its opening on the south. It has two sections separated by a step. The little room measures 5.7 ft x 4.9 ft. It is decorated with a mosaic panel with a christological monogram on a lower level than the floor of the entrance. A border of masonry runs along the western wall. The walls probably fell down when the Crusader Basilica was built, but still have traces of four to six layers of plaster. Frs. Testa and Antonucci undertook a most patient task and made it possible to recover some graffiti scratched by pilgrims on the top layer oof plaster. This made visible the original plaster and that certainly is the most interesting. When the third coat (beginning from the rock itself) of plaster was removed a coin was found in the mortar. It came from the middle of the 4th century, perhaps from Emperor Constant. The small coin is an excellent archaeological instrument for dating the original decoration at least. It is decorated with a continuous series of flowery twigs together with a crown. There is an inscription in a red colored

30. Detail of the fresco of Paradise in the Grotto of Conon.

colored rose in the middle of the composition and it mentions the lady benedactor, Valeria. Iconographically, while the twigs refer to the theme of "paradise" as a pleasant place of reward and happiness, the crown is connected with the victory that has been achieved. According to the interpretation of Frs. Bagatti and Testa, the border represents paradise as a reward for the christian life led by a nameless martyr venerated alongside the Grotto. Various graffiti with invocations to Jesus the Christ scratched in nearby areas of the crown give testimony to the veneration which pre-crusader pilgrims had for this place.

Two steps carved into the rock connect the corridor in front of the two grottos with a section of mosaic which lies to the south of a slightly elevated platform. The section of mosaic still visible, ornamented with a cross within a crown and with crosses scattered throughout the section is lined up facing the Grotto, just like the mosaic of Conon. Fr. Bagatti makes the conclusion that this must be due to an arrangment which was prior to the building of the Byzantine church. In that one the central and northern naves would correspond with a new mosaic which normally faced to the east.

Still visible from the Byzantine basilica are the three naves (64 ft long and 26.2 ft wide) of the central apse and fragments of the mosaic of the north and south nave. The sacred area including the basilica, the atrium on the west and the annexed monastery on the south, extended beyond the southern walls of the present basilica and covered an area 157.4 ft long and 88.5 ft wide. Of the whole pile of mosaics used to decorate a place of this type 82 pieces used in the building have been recovered and it indicates that a synagogue-like building must have been erected in the vicinity of the Grotto. Father Bagatti thinks that they could be part of the pillar of the Byzantine church which in the present liturgical arrangement form the support of the mensa which surrounds the altar of celebration in front of the Grotto. The area where the altar is has been made by lowering the original level of the central nave of the Byzantine church. Under the mosaic of the corona with the monogram a basin was found with steps carved out in the rock so as to make it part of the original religious use of the area opposite the Grotto.

A wrought iron fence decorated with various symbols (H. Pedit) separates the Grotto from the area around it. A guard-railing with gilt copper relief portraying the Annunciation and angels bowing down encircles the area from above. (C. Colruyt). On the sides of the Grotto two pillars from the Crusader basilica are still visible. Alongside the bannister which surrounds the sacred area there are two wrought iron candlesticks (A. Gerardi).

31. Detail of the mosaic of the early shrine with the monogram in a wreath.

32. A basin (foreground) under the mosaic floor in front of the Grotto of the Annunciation and the Grotto of Conon.

The altar in the central apse of the basilica is adorned with a copper crucifix (Ben Shalom). The north apse has on its walls two bas relieves of saints Joachim and Anna, parents of Mary and grand-

parents of Jesus. In the southern apse the picture of the Annunciation (17th century) is kept. At one time it was hanging on the altar of the Grotto in the Franciscan Church.

33. The altar for concelebrations in front of the Grotto of the Annunciation.

UNAM
CATHOLICAM

VI

THE UPPER BASILICA

The two spiral staircases in the front part of the basilica lead from the lower church to the upper church. They are lighted by stained glass windows showing Marian themes (A. Farina).

The gigantic open space used for the celebrations of the upper church is brightly illuminated by the cupola made of prefabricated panels and by the wide windows in the facade, the walls (Ingrand), and under the tambour of the cupola (Yoki Aebischer). On the wall in back of the sanctuary the spacious mosaic drawing on the theme of the *one, holy, catholic,* and *apostolic* church (S. Fiume) stands out prominently, together with some writings on themes of the *Apocalypse* (Gl. Baruzzi).

The north side chapel highlights Franciscan Saints. Some of them are shown with their relics encased with a silver border within their portrait. Also displayed are the apostolic labors

34. Major altar with mosaic background on the theme of the One, Holy, Catholic and Apostolic Church (Salvator Fiume).

35. Inside the Upper Basilica with the pillars which support the large central cupola.

36. Inlaid floor around the oculus which commemorates the prerogotives of the Blessed Mother expressed in the Ecumenical Councils and by Popes.

of the Custody of the Holy Land (Gl. Baruzzi). The chapel of the Blessed Sacrament on the south side developes the themes of war and peace and the conflict between good and evil (R. Ubeda).

The pictures on the side walls are a collection of scenes of the veneration of the Blessed Virgin in the main shrines of the world.

On the right wall are: Camerun — Hungary — Brazil — United States — Poland — Spain — Italy.

And on the left wall are: England — Australia — Argentina — Venezuela — Lebanon — Japan — Canada.

Above the confession stations against the western wall are four inlaid representations of God's mercy in giving pardon to sinners (Alessandrini).

The plaques of the 14 Stations of the Cross (A. Biancini) are attached to

the pilars which support the cupola. At the back entrance to the upper Basilica there is a touching memorial to Pope John XXIII who approved the designs of the new basilica. Just before the gate leading into the area of the oculus, is the memorial to the pilgrimage of Pope Paul VI and inside in the inlaid marble floor are some of the prerogatives of the Blessed Virgin. They are expressed in the phrases of the deliberations of ecumenical councils and in the words of Popes. They extend from the divine motherhood taught by the council of Ephesus to the proclamation of the dogma of the Assumption (Pius XII, 1950).

Nearby the sanctuary a bronze candelabra (9.5 ft) narrates the story of salvation from Adam and Eve to Jesus, the Redeemer who upholds and presents to the world the boat of Peter which today is under the leadership of the Pope (A. Farina).

The two doors on the north wall lead from the upper basilica to the courtyard outside the church. There the floor pavement stretches over and covers

37. Annunciation stained-glass windows by Max Ingrand.
38. Camerun Mosaic. Our Lady of Africa.

the outside ruins of the ancient village. *The baptistry* rises above the platform. On its bronze shutters (N. Steenbergan) are the themes of sacred history connected with the Church from the Circumcision (western door, with the Tree of Jesse, the Annunciation, the adoration of the shepherds and the calling of Peter) and the Church from the Gentiles (western door with the cycle of Jonah the Prophet, the adoration of the Magi, Pentecost and the calling of Paul). In the two lunettes are set the Nativity and the adoration of the Magi in glass terracotta (A. Biancini).

The Hartmann husband-wife team produced the colored windows, wall mosaics and bronze font of Jesus' baptism in the baptistry. The designs of the courtyard floor (canticle of the creatures and the Franciscan coat of arms) are the creation of Elias Tabry of Nazareth and executed by A. Alessandrini.

At the top of the pyramid above the sanctuary of the upper basilica there is a life size group in copper of Calvary (Galvanoni). Seven bells dedicated to the Crucifixion, Immaculate Conception, the Resurrection, St. Francis, Sts. Joachim and Ann and St. Justin make up the Basilica concert which three times a day rings out the Ave Maria of Nazareth. It is the composition of don Mariano Jaccarino of the Abbey of Montecassino.

39. The Good Shepherd (Adrian Alessandrini).

40. One of the Stations of the Cross (A. Biancini).

41. Baptism of Jesus (Hartmann husban-wife team).

VII

THE RUINS OF THE VILLAGE AND THE MUSEUM

Upon request, a person can visit the underground area of Nazareth north of the Basilica as well as the museum connected with it.

In this area, until 1930 the former Franciscan convent was constructed on the ruins of the episcopal palace of the Crusader times and there still are remnants of its walls. The area shows us clearly how the rocky surface slopes downward to the south. The houses of the village were built on the slope and they made use of an underground basement area. It was easy to carve out needed space in the soft limestone of the hill. The dwellings of the people made of masonry were built above or alongside the grottoes. A real good example of a half stone dwelling can be seen near the side wall of the crusader basilica where the mosaics of the Byzantine monastery

42-43. Statue of St. Peter with keys and a church and a mythical animal of the portal. These two sculptures were to decorate the basilica of the Crusader period. Now they are kept in the Museum.

44. A rock house of the ancient village of Nazareth in the excavated area.

are hanging on display. Opposite them, is still a grotto with a small room with the walls and the entrance carved by chipping them out of the rock. In this grotto, then the basement of the convent visiting room, Fr. Viaud discovered five superb capitals which are now kept in the museum. In the grotto there is still an oven cut into the southwest corner, and some of the silo openings are visible in the floor. Small ring shaped holes carved in the corner edge of the rock and a manger reveal that the grotto was used as an animal stall at least for a certain period of time.

Moving toward the north there is another grotto open on its western side and there were found other mouths of open silos in the floor. The silos are pear-shaped and were used to store grain and other materials. One of the most interesting complexes in the area is the one called the "oil press" which leads to the Grotto of the Annunciation, but is separated by the wall of the basilica.

The museum is located in a large hall of the episcopal palace redesigned to serve this purpose. The main discoveries of the archaeological excavations undertaken before building the present

45. The base of the column with the Ave Maria in Greek carved into it.

46-47. Ave Maria in Greek. Details of the graffiti.

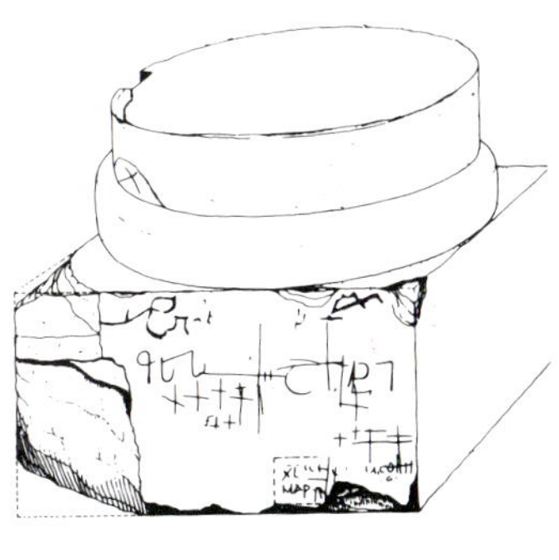

48. "I wrote on the Holy Place of Mary". Graffito in Greek on the plaster of a column.

shrine are on display there. The history of human presence at Nazareth is summarized by means of a few groups of ceramic samples which come from the second millennium B.C. to 1500 A.D. The vessels of Middle Bronze I and II (2000-1600 B.C.) and from Late Bronze 1500-1300 B.C. came from tombs found at the outer south wall of the Crusader basilica. Those of Iron I (X-IX century B.C.) come from a tomb discovered on the slopes of the hill in the west section of the central living area (Mansour house). Iron II (VIII century B.C.) is represented by a jar with a narrow neck with two handles and a funnel which was found in a silo east of the basilica. The lamps and pots of the roman period come from the funerary furniture of the Lahham tomb discovered to the south of the shrine. The glass dishes come from the medieval period down to the XV century and come from a variety of places.

In regards to the history of the shrine some building materials are to be noted which come from a synagogue found under the mosaic of the building from the Byzantine period. Graffiti on the plaster which covers the stones which were cut from the stone from around Nazareth give evidence that Christian pilgrims passed by there and of the veneration they had for the holy place. In the middle of the hall the base of a column with other graffiti is open to

49. The text of the Hail Mary engraved on a piece of building material from the Crusader period.

view. An Armenian expression "beautiful maiden" refers to the Blessed Mother and there is the famous Hail Mary in Greek (*Xaire Maria*). This iscription is the earliest instance of this prayer to the Virgin of Nazareth that archaeology has produced. It has become the most common Marian prayer among all Christians. In two separate cases the stone base of a column is displayed. It has the Greek graffito. *"I wrote on the holy place of M(ary)"* and the panel with the graffito showing a person carrying a cross. In later Byzantine iconography it became the characteriistic figure of St. John the Baptist.

The museum also displays other sculpture pieces used to decorate the Basilica of the Annunciation. they are the most outstanding pieces of Crusader art found in the Holy Land. Among the grotesque animals in the conci molding of the great arch of the Basilica's facade, are to be noted: the lower part of a figure with an ample fold in its garment, perhaps an angel; a fragment with wings; a head broken off at eye level; two feet with sandals. Three pieces of a cornice are fastened on the southern wall. In them it is possible to piece together part of an inscription in superb small Latin letters: "(Behold the Hand) maid of the Lo(rd)... concei(ved o)f the Holy Spirit". In the corner edge of that same wall a stone inbedded in the crack contains, in small letters of the 12th Century, the

50. The Church which encourages an apostle in preaching the word of God (dis. G. Tilia).

51. Below is a detail of the door of the Basilica of the Crusader period.

first part of the Hail Mary in Latin.

In a small apse along the northern wall, the axed statue of St. Peter has been set up to view. It was found on 22 June, 1966 while the north wall of the Franciscan church was being taken down. The apostle is wearing a tunic and a mantle tucked in at the waist with a cord. In his right hand he is clasping two large keys and in his left hand he holds a small model of a church with three apses and a steeple on top. In a rectangular section of the same wall five capitals are on display which P. Viaud discovered in 1909 hidden in the cave called grotto of the "Capitals". They were concealed by an anonymous and well intentioned devotee of art after the fall of the Latin kingdom of Jerusalem.

The capital of the church is in the middle. Under the baldachino adorned with architectural motifs which are repeated in the other capitals, is a figure of a woman with a crown on her head facing to the right. In her right hand she holds a longshafted cross and with her left she is pulling along a barefooted apostle. On both sides there is a demon armed with a shield, spear and arrow ready to attack the defenseless pair. The artist intended to personify Faith or the Church which leads the apostle in preaching in spite of opposition from the demons.

Capital of St. Thomas. It is one of the four octagonal capitals, the first one on the right. In the middle of four pairs of apostles is the risen Jesus, with a cross in his halo. he is showing the wound of the spear in his side to the unbelieving apostle.

52-53. The Risen Jesus appears to the Apostles in the Cenacle (dis. G. Tilia).

54-55. Capital of St. Peter. The call of Peter (right). St. Peter raises Tabitha (dis. G. Tilia).

Capital of St. Peter. Here there are two scenes from the life of the Apostle. They are Peter walking on water (Mt. 14, 22-33) and Peter restoring life to Tabitha (Acts, 9, 36-43), with the standing figure of Christ in the middle of the scene.

56-57. Capital of St. James the Greater (dis. G. Tilia).

Capital of St. James the Greater. Fr. Bagatti suggests reading it from the left to the right. It is the legendary life of the Apostle as told in the Latin Apocryphal Acts of Pseudo-Abdia (VI Century). While he was preaching to the Jews, James converted a certain Phileto who witnessed some of the Apostle's miracles. One of them was the cure of a woman possessed by devils. James who had founded the local church, is shown on this capital as a bishop with the tiara and as a deacon, was persecuted by Hermogene, by the high priest Abiatar and by the scribe Josia. However, overwhelmed by the facts he became baptized. The apostle paid dearly by a harsh beheading. His tomb was honored by his disciples among whom were Theodore and Anastasius.

58-59. Capital of St. Matthew (dis. G. Tilia).
60. Detail of the Capital of the Church with demon.

Capital of St. Matthew. According to Pseudo-Abdia, in the city of Maddaver in Abyssinia, the apostle Matthew presented by the Eunuch Candace, baptized by the deacon Philip, restored to life Euphranore son of the king Eglippo who then was baptized together with his family, wife, sons (Euphranore and Beeor) and his daughter Iphigenia. When the king died his successor, Irtaco wanted to marry Iphigenia who, however, was consecrated to the Lord. Matthew assisted the girl in her holy intention and gave her the veil of consecrated virgins which she is asking for on her knees in front of all the people. Such action brought on the anger of Irtaco who, encouraged by the devil, condemned the apostle to death. The Christian Beeor succeeded Irtaco and brought peace back to the church. The devils had to leave defeated.

VIII

THE CHURCH OF ST. JOSEPH

The entrance of the church of St Joseph is at the end of the courtyard along the front of the Franciscan Friary. The courtyard is filled with pieces of building materials from the Synagogue, Byzantine and Crusader days. In 1911 the church was reconstructed, according to the Basilica style, on the outline of the Midieval Basilica after the small church of 1858 had been demolished. The shrine, called "the Nutrition," came to be considered the house of Joseph and the Holy Family. Abbot Arculf mentions it in 670: *"The city of Nazareth... sits on a mountain and still has large stone buildings. Two very large churches are there. One is in the center of the city, built on two arches over the place where the house in which Jesus was nourished once stood."*

Inside are the frescoes of A. Della Torre, the stain glass windows of

61. The church of St. Joseph reconstructed in 1911.

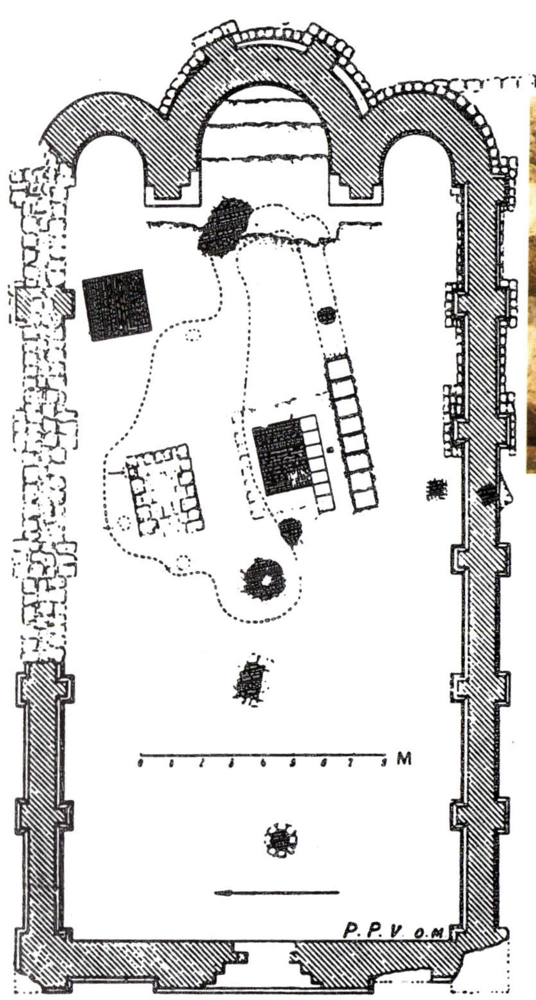

J. Gruber, a painting of the Holy Family by F. Lafond and the carpenter apprentice Jesus in the shop of Joseph by Hermmerlain di Vienna.

The floor of the central nave of the church has been elevated so that the antiquities of the Byzantine and Pre-Byzantine period can be seen. They were discovered in various excavations in the area and published by Fr. Viaud.

That the basin was used for baptismal purposes is explained by the following indications: The number seven in the steps is connected with the Judeo-Christian doctrine of the ascent and descent of Jesus and the gifts of the Holy Spirit which come with baptism. The canal is symbolically related to the Jordan River which is crossed to enter into the promised land and through baptism into the church. The rock is a type of symbol of the identification of the baptized person with Christ, the rock and foundation of the church. The squares in the mosaic are like a reminder of the presence of the six protoktistai or first created angels who are always at attention to assist Christ the Redeemer.

Assuming a liturgical use of the basin, the excavation of the cistern for water, the enlargement of the underground grotto and the connecting corridor would explain why the preexisting silos were destroyed so that it could be a place for Baptism. The first part of the

62-63-64. Plan of the church of St. Joseph during the Crusader period. Oldest ruins discovered in the underground area. Possibly a Judeo-Christian baptismal basin and a grotto adapted from silos of the Roman times.

ceremony, connected with the symbolism of light-darkness, would have taken place in the underground grotto. The cistern would have assured the supply of water for baptism.

IX

THE FOUNTAIN OF THE VIRGIN AND THE CHURCH OF ST. GABRIEL

There are two known natural water sources in Nazareth. A small one springs up near the Mensa Christi, and the more abundant Fountain of the Virgin lies north of the village on the road to Tiberias.

This spring flows out of the rock a little above the Fountain, in the church of St. Gabriel. There, from a collecting basin the water runs through an underground system into a first room, then it is channeled below the church and then is collected in a vat before it empties out from the spouts of the monument built along the street. The Russian Abbot Daniel, is the first one who mentions a

65. Inside the Church of St. Gabriel. The spring of Nazareth is in the crypt.

66. The public water spring outside the church of St. Gabirel.

THE ANNUNCIATION

[*10,1*] *During a meeting of the priests, they said: — Let us make a curtain for the temple of the Lord. — The priest said: — Find a spotless maiden for me from the tribe of David. — The ministers went out, searched and found seven maidens. The priest recalled the youthful maiden Mary, that she was of the tribe of David and spotless in the sight of God. The ministers left and brought her in.*

[*10.2*] *So they brought her into the temple of the Lord, and the priest said: — Cast lots for the maiden who spins gold, asbestos, bisso, silk, hyacinth, scarlet and genuine purple. Purple and scarlet were assigned to Mary. She took them and returned home. At that moment Zachary became deaf: until he spoke again, Samuel took his place. Mary took the scarlet and wove it.*

round church dedicated to the Archangel Gabriel near the fountain and ties it in with the Annunciation: *"Then we left the city and we went toward the east side and we found a well worth noting and very deep with cool water to which there were steps going down. A round church, dedicated to the Archangel Gabriel, covers this well... It was there, near the well, that the holy Virgin received the first Annunciation of the Archangel".* This is probably a transposition to Nazareth of a page from the Gospel of James which makes the meeting of the angel with the Virgin take place near the spring. The church with the spring was mentioned by Focas in 1177. The western pilgrims such as Saewulf and Theodoric in addition to the church also describe the monument at the spring, decorated on the outside with marble and sculptures. "In the same city" writes Theodoric "a spring wells up through a marble conduit in the shape of a lion. From this spring the boy Jesus used to fetch water and carry it to His mother", which is probably a reference to a passage in the Gospel of Thomas.

The modern church on top of the ancient chapel was built in 1750 by the Greek-Orthodox monks who still officiate there. The wooden iconastis done by Andrea Maistu and installed there in 1767 ranks among the valuable icons of the school of Jerusalem. In 1977-78 two Rumanian artists, Michel and Gabriel Marosan added the scenes of the Old and New Testament on the walls.

[11,1] *She took the jar and went to draw water. A voice then said: — Rejoice, O full of grace, the Lord is with you, blessed are you among women. — She looked around, right and left, to where the voice came from. Trembling all over she went home, put the jar down, took the purple, sat on her bench and began to weave.* [2] *Suddenly an angel of the Lord appeared before her and said:*
[*11,2*] *Fear not, Mary, for you have found favor before the Master of all things, and you will conceive through his word. — But she, hearing this, was perplexed, thinking: — Must I conceive by the word of the living Lord God and then give birth like all other women give birth?*

[*11,3*] *The angel of the Lord said: — Not so Mary! The power of the Lord with his shadow will cover you. Therefore the holy one born of you will be called Son of the Most High. You will give Him the name Jesus for he will save his people from their sins. — Mary replied: — Behold the handmaid of the Lord. Let His word come upon me.*

(Protogospel of James)

X

OTHER SHRINES

The cemetery at the Dames de Nazaret

One of the cemeteries on the slope of the hill of Nazareth opposite the wadi in front of the Basilica of the Annunciation is the one in the underground area of the convent of the Dames de Nazaret. There a well preserved example of a *kokhim* (oven) type burial room with its closing stone, from the Roman period, can be inspected.

A medieval building was erected over this site which shows traces of another Roman tomb. Also still earlier ancient graves were changed later on to make a cistern.

67. A tomb from the 1st century with its closing stone, discovered under the convent of the Dames of Nazaret.

The synagogue or school of Christ.

This stands near the Greek Catholic church built in 1882. The "synagogue" is composed of a single medieval hall which had been used as a church by the Greek Catholic community since 1741. Already at that time the hall was called "the Synagogue".

68. Inside the so-called "Synagogue" served by the Greek Catholic community.

The church of St. Anthony Abbot

This was built in 1774 for the Maronite community of Nazareth.

69. Inside the "Mensa Christi".

The mensa Christi or Balata

In 1860 The Franciscans, using the design of Fra Serafino da Roccascalegna, put up the chapel enclosing a section of rock which Quaresimi describes "like a rock flat and round... called by the natives Mensa Christi because it is believed that Christ ate there with his disciples, even after his resurrection... Under the rock a spring of living water splashes forth".

In the vicinity of the chapel two tombs of the roman epoc were discovered. One of them has ten kokhim.

The chapel of the Trembling

On the hill where now there is a rest house and the convent of the Poor Clares, medieval travellers mention a chapel of St. Zachary. Fra Niccolò da Poggibonsi says that there was a "fine monastery and inside it there is a church which is called Holy Mary of the Fright", recalling the episode of Luke 4, 29-30, located a bit farther up in the valley. The chapel was restored by the Franciscans around 1880 and made over again in 1972.

70. Inside the chapel of the Trembling.

71. The mountain called "Precipation".

The Precipation

The "commemoratorium de casis Dei" mentions that a mile distant from Nazareth to the south there was a monastery with a church in honor of the Virgin where they used to show "the place where the Jews wanted to cast Jesus down headlong". The ruins of a church and a rocky area with at least some traces of a mosaic floor visible among the rocks of the mountain in front of Jebel el-Qasfe, are the remains of the monastery or hermitage still there today.

The Church of St. Ann at Seforis

The Pilgrim of Piacenza (570) says that he visited Seforis-Diocesarea, the ancient capital of Galilee before Tiberias on the lake was founded. It was "the cruet and basket of Holy Mary. Here was the chair she was using when the angel came to her".

These Marian memories were given new life during the days of the Crusaders who constructed a basilica dedicated to St. Ann, the mother of the Blessed Virgin.

Every year the Franciscans from their Friary in Nazareth make a pilgrimage there. In 1841 they were able to take possession of the ruins of the basilica.

In 1908 Father Prospero Viaud removed the later superstructures from over the wall ruins of the basilica. It became clear, in susbsequent excavations that the Christian shrine had been constructed over the remains of a synagogue structure with mosaics. In one Hebrew inscription the donor's name is legible: Rabbi Yudah, son of Tanhum.

East of the church, the Sisters of St. Ann built a school which is still active today. An Israel-American archaeological mission began excavations in recent years in the upper section of the hill. They discovered splendid mosaics dating from the Roman and Byzantine periods.

72. Seforis. The apse section of the basilica of St. Ann dating to the Crusader days (12th century).

Septentrion

NAZARETH

XI

FRANCISCANS AT NAZARETH

Patient Wait — Stormy Presence

The earliest mention of the existence of a Franciscan convent at Nazareth is that of Friar Bartholomew da Pisa. Around 1390 he wrote: "in Nazaret fuit etiam locus (Fratum Minorum), etsi modo ob pravitatem saracenorum sit dimissus". The validity of this reference, even more so since it is not supported by other sources, leaves us perplexed about its real historical value. But still it is certain that the Friars during those centuries toward the end of the middle ages, whenever possible would not pass up an opportunity to pilgrimage to Nazareth. And to have Franciscans seen at this place at this time would be very, very useful.

To find a Franciscan presence at Nazareth that is both historically and juridically certain we must go to the fifth decade of the 16th century. Fr. Boniface of Ragusa, twice Custos of Terra Santa, wrote in 1567 that about

73. The village of Nazareth in 1664, as recalled by Fr. Eugène Roger.

twenty years earlier the Friars were at Nazareth where they took care of the church of the Annunciation. At a certain point in time, on account of uprisings in the country they had to flee to Jerusalem, but left the key with a Christian of the place "who until now takes care of the house, opens and closes the church and keeps the two lamps burning with the oil which Father Custos gives him".

There exists moreover a firman, a royal decree of the Sultan, which the Father Superior of Terra Santa obtained on June 15, 1546, that allowed the Franciscans to restore their church of Nazareth. Evidently it refers to the Crusader church of the Annunciation, but already at the end of 1200 it was "practically completely destroyed" and from then on it was seen in that condition by pilgrims. Unfortunately the courageous attempt of the Franciscans could not be achieved, because, as has been seen, very soon they had to leave Nazareth. The contemporary F. Gonzaga notes that in spite of this fact the Custody of the Holy Land continued to maintain its rights in Nazareth. Not to be forgotten, though, is the fact that among the ruins, there more or less always remained a veneration for a grotto in that place, as the earthly site of the gospel.

1620: The Franciscans at Nazareth for good

It was only in 1620 that the Franciscans, once and for all, were able to

74. Fr. Tommaso Obicini da Novara.

75. Description of taking possession of the shrine written by Father Tommaso Obicini da Novara (ed. 1628).

QVOMODO SANCTAM, ET VENERABILEM NAZARETH ECCLESIAM

Quæ per multa annorum curricula deserta, & derelicta manserat, his diebus à Sydoniorum Principe, Reuerendus Pater Frater Thomas à Nouaria, ordinis Min. Regularis Obseruantiæ, Sacri Montis Sion Guardianus, diligenter procurarit; gratisq; sibi, ac suæ Religionis Fratribus obtentam die 29. Decembris, anno Domini 1620. in veram iuris possessionem receperit, postremò verò, qualiter restaurauerit, Monasteriumq; sui ordinis ibi extruxerit, latè explicatur.

CVIVS OCCASIONE REI, NOVA ETIAM aliqua, scitu, memoriaque digna illic ad corroborandam Sanctæ Lauretanæ Domus veritatem, adinuenta afferuntur, & similiter miracula quædam, quippè quæ Deus Benedictus ad Genitricis suæ gloriam, & fidei nostræ incrementum, in loco, vbi verbum caro factum est, dispensatione mirabili, ipsis etiam infidelibus quotidiè operatur sincerè, fideliterque hic ab eodem enarrantur. Vna cum Processione, celebranda ibidem: quotidiè post Completorium ab eodem R. P. edita.

VENETIIS, M DC XXIII.

Apud Misserinum. Superiorum Permissu.

76. Druse Emir of Lebanon, Fakhreddin.

77. Decree ordered by Fakhreddin which legally authorized the Franciscans to possess the shrine of the Annunciation (1624).

settle in Nazareth. It was Fr. Tommaso Obicini da Novara, Custos of the Holy Land, who decided to take advantage of those years when Lebanon and Upper Galilee (including the area of Nazareth) were governed in a rather autonomous way by the Druse Emir Fakhreddin, who was kindly disposed to the Christians, to move toward recovering the shrine of Nazareth. This Fr. Tommaso, accompanied by the French Counsel of Sidon and some European merchants, in the early part of the summer of 1620, approached the Emir Fakhreddin and explained the advantages of his intention. The idea sat well with the Emir and he not only gave his approval, but freely agreed to whatever Fr. Custos requested. In addition he also gave a substantial amount of money for the first needs of the Friars who would be settled at Nazareth. And so that this concession would have public juridical validity, the Emir arranged that the Cadì of Safed, on whom the administration of the area of Nazareth depended, should send the document granting the deeded title of the property to the Friars of Terra Santa. This document is preserved in the Archives of the Custody of the Holy Land in Jerusalem.

So, finally, on December 19, 1620 the Custos, Fr. Tommaso Obicini went in person to take possession of the shrine of the Annunciation at Nazareth,

DOCUMENT

Wakf "Donation" of the Grotto of Nazareth

...Praise to Him to Whom is due praise and thanks and prayer and peace be upon his Prophet, the most noble of all creation, upon his family and his Companions keeping to the straight path.

This is the document of a waqf (gift), authentic, legal, binding, written down and valid up to this present moment. It comes from the person who decreed this edict. Its content, interpretation and prescription are to be understood accordingly. In agreement with our gracious law and with the assembly of the eminent and illustrious tarìqa of the mighty and fortified stronghold of Safed — may the Eternal God watch over it — in the presence of our most learned Lord, faithful, most intelligent governor hanifita who affixed his own signature to the upper part of this document, we now present Signor Jean from the Frankish Community. He is the legal procurator on behalf of James, the Frenchman, who represents the community subject to the wishes of our Lord the Sultan — May the Lord God strengthen his throne and prolong his reign! The proxi status of the aforementioned Jean exists in virtue of legal and oral instruments, and is still valid according to the testimony of the two dhimmi (guarantors) David, son of Elias the tailor, from the community of the Jews of Safed presently residing in Sidon, and of David, son of Menahèm the Jew perfumer at Sidon, from whom it is evident that the aforesaid James has given proxy in the transcribed legal form to the Jean already referred to, to receive in waqf that which he had built by his own hand and at his own expense and good will on the solid place over the grotto which is in the village of Nazareth used by the Frank Christians for their visits and which has been theirs from ancient times to the present day for their visits. A place has been made there for the veneration of Mary, mother of the Lord Jesus — may the prayer and peace of God descend upon our Prophet and those under him — and they always go there to visit this grotto. On this basis the legal governor has granted to this James of Vendome the building; and in virtue of the perpetual order of our lord the Sultan — May the merciful God watch over him! —...

This waqf has therefore become a legal waqf, binding and in force: it shall not be either changed or substituted in any of its single parts...

This legal deed was dictated at the end of the month of Dhù'l-Qa'da of year 1043.

(From the legal document of the Cadì of Safed)

DOCUMENT

Official possession of the Holy Grotto

In the year of the Lord 1620, after I had obtained credential letters from the Prince of the city of Sidon and everything else regarding the settlement of the affairs from the Cadi of Safed, I was accompanied by a certain Chiaual, Governor of Safed, and during the whole journey, also by an escort of soldiers together with Fra Giacomo di (Vendome), Priest, and Brother Francesco Salice, a Sicilian and the witnesses which will be recorded below. We all arrived safe and sound at the holy place of Nazareth on November 29, a Sabbath day. There we presented the letters of the Prince and the decrees of the Cadi and completed the reading in the presence of the witnesses amid great joy for everyone, both among ourselves as well as among them and on the very same day we officially took free possession of the right to this Shrine, in the presence of trustworthy witnesses in the person of Signor Oliverio Chiaual, ex-consul of Sidon, Signor Alberto Gardana, former counsel, Signor Francesco Lebar, Procurator of the holy places who came to share with us such tremendous, memorable and holy joy. We entered into the holy place on whose foundations rested the House of Lorreto. We entered into the Holy Grotto where the angel greeted the Blessed Virgin Mary, with much piety and devotion, and we honored it as if we were seeing the Word Incarnate with our own eyes.

Afterwards we set about to clean those ruins, so worthy and that Shrine so famous. We blessed that most ancient altar of the Annunciation erected by Christians. We decorated the holy place with lamps. We lit up the grotto, which was somewhat dark, with lamps and finally, having prepared all things for the divine service, we solemnly sang the Vespers of the sabbath of the last Sunday of Advent. When Vespers and Compline were finished some Arabs who lived at Nazareth, both Moslems and Christians came along. They told us one after the other about extraordinary things which were worth recording. They were things which had been handed down to them by their forefathers and they insisted that what they said was authentic. Every day they spoke to us about miracles which God had continually performed through the intercession of the Virgin Mary... I appointed as custodian of the Holy House of Nazareth the aforementioned Father James, companion on the journey, charging him to take care of the new Convent, mentioning, among other things that miracles should be verified, and above all to try to restore the place. The next day, early in the morning, in all haste I left Nazareth and arrived at Jerusalem after three days.

(Narrated by Fr. Tomaso Obicini da Novara)

by now reduced to "relics" compared to what it must have been in its day. The picturesque but effective image is from the famous Roman traveller Pietro Della Valle who saw the place in April, 1616. The first concern of the Friars, under the leadership of the dynamic first Guardian of Nazareth, Fr. James de Vendôme, was to clean up the holy Grotto and improve it so better services could be celebrated and also to arrange for a small convent nearby as well as adequate accomodations for hosting pilgrims.

As long as they continued to be under the watchful eye of the Emir Fakhreddin, the Friars were able to maintain themselves quite well on the whole. And that made it possible for them to develop a rudimentary apostolate. But the tragic end of their illustrious and munificent benefactor, killed at Constantinople on April 13, 1635 ushered in an era of continual hardships of every sort which lasted for almost two centuries. Truly it was Divine Providence that inspired the Custos, Fr. Diego da Sanseverino to establish a hospice in 1629 at Acre. A city on the sea, fairly near, with a colony of European merchants and the seat of several Consulates of Christian States, it proved to be an excellent temporary refuge for the religious who were forced, not infrequently, to leave Nazareth either because of the outrage of the civil authorities of the place or from an uprising of the people. Here is not the place to discuss each of these forced "flights" from Nazareth.

For the XVII century it will be enough to illustrate how life existed, according to an ancient narrative, even though it is exaggerated: "This Holy House (that is how they called the Nazareth Shrine) from 1620 to 1682 was frequently sacked, burned, destroyed and abandoned; and our poor Friars suffered, death here, imprisonment there and clubbings along with a thousand other forms of molestation and indignities. With all this Terra Santa always restored the place and saw to it that there were some of their people there so that opportune service of God would be maintained, just like is done today".

Among the various sackings that caused very much damage, the one in 1708 is to be especially noted. One memory of it is the following: "In the year of the Lord 1708 the Holy House of Nazareth was sacked and plundered by beduins and natives of the place to such an extent that only the walls were left and nothing else..."

Two years later, exactly on February 2, 1710 the Custos, Fr. Lorenzo Cozza could inform Propaganda Fide that "Once again compensation has been made as much as possible (to the convent of Nazareth for the damaging depredations); so now they have eight religious there and are functioning just as before".

To complete the picture, there was still another flight with the consequent forced and temporary abandonment of the shrine and convent. That happened when Napoleon broke off his siege of Acre and returned to Egypt in 1799. A massacre followed and the Friars fled across the mountains into Lebanon.

As a result of this historical turn of events the Friars embarked upon a most curious activity! It is actually unique rather than rare, in the whole history of Franciscanism. As early as 1697, the Friars debated over a method by which they could effectively retain the precious ruins, because their existence there and their control of the shrine had always

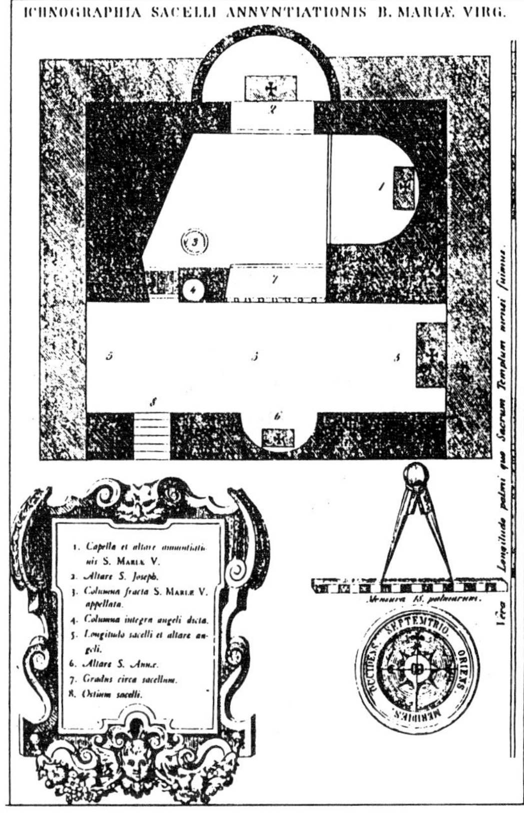

78. The original small church of the Annunciation in a drawing by Father Francesco Quaresmi (1626).

79. Chapel of the Annunciation (Le Bruyn, 1714).

been tenuous. So they thought about "taking a lease out on the village of Nazareth. This seemed to be the only way to maintain and preserve the Holy House of Nazareth." This legal action was repeated again in 1700. With a few interruptions this lasted until 1770. Soon enough, however, three other nearby villages, Jaffo, Migdal and Kneifes, came to be included in the lease. For all practical purposes this "lease" (in the Latin documents "conductio" was used) made the Father Guardian of Nazareth the only civil official in these four villages. As such, he administered justice, levied taxes on the people, but always in dependence on the Pasha of Sidon and of the "Leader" of Acre. Attached to the office was an enormous annual fee. This system is reminiscent, in some ways, of some feudal systems of medieval Europe.

Did this scheme, devised to maintain control of Nazareth more firmly prove satisfactory? On the whole it seems that it did, simply because of its duration. Special times and places need their own solutions. But we should note that very little about this situation was published, and even so, what we have is quite fragmentary.

When the general political situation significantly changed in the middle of the last century, the Franciscan presence at Nazareth was able to be expanded into the flourishing works that during past epochs could not even be thought of. A date to remember for the convent and for the Custody of Terra Santa would be the canonical opening of the Novitiate at Nazareth on April 1, 1867 where it remained, with a few exceptions, until 1940.

80 Door of the church in 1730.

Since, as we have seen, Acre was, in a certain way, the salvation of the Franciscan Nazareth, during its days it was this very Nazareth that became the center of Catholic influence in the whole of Galilee, and even the matrix and stronghold of Catholicism in the region down to our modern times.

It was the custom of the Orientals who inhabit the slopes of mountains to transform the grottos or rocks into cool rooms to avoid the summer heat. At the entrance of these hollow spaces they build their houses in such a way that they can move from one part to the other. The House of Loreto was thus constructed in front of the second chapel of the Shrine of Nazareth, which originally was a natural grotto or one artificially carved into the rock. Now it is changed into an Oratory. It was reenforced with walls all covered with marble so that the vault, 11 feet high with the arch of a same height, was formed out of the same natural rock. The Grotto is square in shape; the floor, however, once covered with mosaic, now is of marble slabs. The entrance of the Holy House of Loreto was originally closed with a screen, but now is open to everyone day and night and the entrance is through two arches... On the Eastern side the very ancient Altar of the Annunciation of the Blessed Virgin Mary is placed; the rest is of recent construction, done after the Holy Place was ransomed. It can be argued that the ancient Christians, with this altar wanted to indicate to future ages that in this grotto and not elsewhere the greeting of the Angel to the Blessed Virgin took place, she who through the power of the Holy Spirit conceived the Saviour. The fact is further confirmed by the column which is situated on the western side and suspended from the rocky ceiling to point out the exact spot where the Blessed Virgin Mary was when she spoke with the Angel about the tremendous mystery of the Conception of the Lord. In front, at the center of the Grotto there is a small place hemispherical in shape, eleven feet long from west to east and seven in width, north to south. In that place, at one time, there was the altar dedicated to St. Joseph which was removed to build the stairs which the Friars cut into the rock to make it serviceable. There they built walls above the entrance where they put up a beautiful door made from the ancient ruins. This little den is rather dark even though there is a door on the eastern side. Actually this door is closed by a large wooden chest decorated on the inside with inlaid gold flowers. In the center there is the altar of the Annunciation of the Blessed Virgin Mary. Its lower part is completely empty, without the usual antipendium. The box has been placed in the Grotto in a pentagonal shape... At the bottom of this there is a star made of marble with 24 points... which visitors of the place kiss with great devotion.

(Fr. E. Horn: "Ichnographiae Monumentorum Terra Sanctae" — 1725/1744

Now let us list what has been accomplished to date.

Solicitous care of the Shrine of the Annunciation and of its liturgical services

When the Franciscans arrived in Nazareth, December 19, 1620, inspite of the inclement season, a quick refurbishing of at least a part of the ruins was necessary so that they could be of some use if only temporarily. As soon as possible Fr. Jacques de Vendôme built "on top of the foundations where the Holy Laurentana (sic) House was, another church", or better he put up a building in front of the Holy Grotto joining the two together, so as to have a more spacious ambient-church. This church was blessed by the Custos Fr. Paolo da Lodi on June 29, 1632 "under the title of the Name Jesus". How this first arrangement of the church (and convent) of Nazareth looked are illustrated by some prints of that 17th century.

A century later, since the church

FROM THE CHRONICLES OF TERRA SANTA

The building of this church brought much consolation to all our Catholics because they had erected the most beautiful, majestic, and prayerful church which the Holy See possessed in these parts of the East. But it was a hurt to the schismatic heretics and, filled with anger they spread the word that we had built here in Nazareth, not really a church in honor of the most holy Mary, but rather a huge fortress for the Christian Princes. Through this calumny even the Minister of the Turks was moved to join with a Capigi who was in this part of the country to visit this building. Very Reverend Fr. Guardian was advised of this fact and it seemed right for him to be present at this inquiry to stand up for the rights of the Shrine and put down the calumnies of the schismatics. And so paying no attention to the evident perils he was exposing himself to, for at that time the road was infested with robbers, he set out around October 10, 1730 for Nazareth in the company (of Fr. Procurator and two other religious)...; *as soon as they had gone one league from the Holy City, they were for the first time surrounded by villains for a bit of maltreatment and a bit of money; after they walked yet another fair stretch of the countryside, for a second time they had to submit to a more severe mistreatment and subjected to greater tyranny; but they did reach the village called El Bir..., in that place there was such deplorable hostility and they found themselves surrounded by more than*

81. Remains of the tabernacle, work of F. Rauzino (1734).

was "in a condition of ruin beyond repair" it became necessary to think of a new one. With immense industry and ingenuity it became possible to set the first stone on May 7,1730 and to finish the undertaking in only six months. On October 15 of that same year, 1730, the Custos Fr. Peter da Luri came "to the shrine of Nazareth with a large number not only of our Catholics, but also of heretics and Turks, and blessed the new church with appropriate ceremonies".

Another century and a half later, more basic work came about. Actually,

---

200 Arabs and Scoundrels who clubbed them, plundered them, and dragged them on the ground; and they would surely have been left to a certain death in that place except that from that blessed fountain where the freshest water was gushing out, there came along two women warning those scoundrels to stop the outrage against the poor, innocent Religious, saying that their blood would seek revenge before God on their sons, at which they ceased their outrageous behaviour, but not before exacting many piasters which they had with them for paying the camel drivers for their services. And even though it was suggested to the Very Reverend that they should return back to avoid other similar unpleasant encounters, it seemed more important to him that the Shrine of Nazareth should be defended than his own life, he continued his journey so wounded, and half dead as he was, with his companions.

On Sunday, October 15, a large number of people came to the Shrine of Nazareth. They included not only our Catholic people, but also many heretics and Turks. In the presence of all he blessed the new Church with solemn ceremonies, and during the day he confirmed more than 100 Catholics. The man named Sir Knight Isnardi always assisted him in these ceremonies. On Monday, the 16th, the Officials accompanied by the Capigi, presented themselves to visit the building. The entire event redounded to our great glory because after that it was declared that indeed the place was not a fortress, but a real Church and dwelling place for Religious and that done at the expense of many piasters. The cost of that building amounted to sixty thousand piasters.

82. The outside of the Shrine of the Annunciation after the construction done in 1877.

in 1877, it was deemed necessary to lengthen the old church by 32.8 ft. and to make other improvements in the other parts of the building. This included adding a modest belltower which was lacking in the first. All this work was undertaken by the then Commissary of the Holy Land in Venice, Fr. Cipriano da Treviso.

The shrine-church of Nazareth continued to be unsatisfactory in every way, even after the building project of 1877. So, when the World War ended, ideas of a really suitable Basilica were discussed. When the Holy Father, Pius XI was informed of these thoughts, "His Holiness [concurred] whole heartedly and added his encouragement to the holy undertaking."

In 1954, on the occasion of the First Centenary of the proclamation of the dogma of the Immaculate Conception, Father Custos Hyacinth Faccio and the Discretorium of Terra Santa decided "to get started on the construction of the new Basilica of the Annunciation at Nazareth." Once more so many serious difficulties surfaced that the project as planned had to be suspended. On March 2, 1959 the final approval

83. Painting of the Annunciation in the Grotto (18th Century Spanish School)

arrived. Cardinal Tardini, Vatican Secretary of State, sent the Most Reverend Father August Sépinski, the Minister General "the nihil obstat, from the competent Commission, for the project of the new Shrine of the Annunciation, worked out by the Architect Giovanni Muzio of Milan." It included the permission to begin the construction as soon as the Franciscan Order would be ready to undertake it. After ten years of intense work the basilica of the Annunciation, constructed as it was according to the plans of Muzio, was ready for consecration on March 23, 1969. His Eminence Cardinal Gabriel Garrone, Prefect of the Sacred Congregation of Catholic Education officiated. Present were six Very Reverend Bishops, the Very Reverend Father Constantine Koser, Minister General and the complete General Definitorium.

While the ingenious Architect and the skilled workmen toiled at the Basilica, there was also intensely active work proceeding on another aspect of the project. Fr. Bellarmino Bagatti and Fr. Emmanuel Testa, the renowned international scholars of Jerusalem's Studium Biblicum Franciscanum, noted and recorded every detail of historical archaeology as it surfaced. Thanks to them, a

84. Left to right: Architect Giovanni Muzio, Father Alfonso Calabrese and Father Benedetto Antonucci. They planned, programed and directed the building of the new Basilica.

85. Left to right: Father Bellarmino Bagatti and Father Emmanuel Testa.

new colossal chapter has been added to our historical knowledge, not only of the Boy Jesus, but of the primeval Christianity of Nazareth. This is the charm which delights pilgrims in the streets and lanes of Nazareth. They not only echo the Message of the Angel, but even their stones now are the visible traces of those very first christians who were the family, friends and neighbors, the fellow citizens of Jesus. These stones speak of their daily affairs and way of life!

Now, a church is not vibrant unless it hosts divine services and unless it throbs with the faithful. A 17th century record notes that the Friary at Nazareth was looked upon as one of the four major Friaries of the Custody. In it the Friars celebrated services just like in their other churches. Feasts were celebrated with organ and music, with choir office day and night. Each day, after Compline, hymns and appropriate antiphons helped make the procession inside the church more solemn. Pages from pilgrims' journals give us a fairly complete picture of the Liturgical life at Nazareth. It should be noted that Fr. Tommaso Obicini da Novara went out of his way to introduce that characteristic spiritual tone into the life of the Shrine. He compiled a fitting Procesional which was published in Venice already in 1623, and then republished over and over again until its last edition in 1930. Pilgrims rejoiced in the privilege

18

go Beatissima orans, & credens, nobis Deum hominem dedit vt iam dictum est, Contra hāc columnam ad Orientis latum, Altare à priscis erectum inuenimus, quodque iuxta Ecclesiæ institutum benedicētes, ac in eo deuotè Missarum solemnia celebrantes, primò illud Sanctissimæ Virgini ibi annunciatæ, dedicandum curauimus; Alterum extra specum contra columnam Angeli inter duas Portas a meridie in honorem Archangeli Gabrielis erectum est. Tertium in secretiori speluncæ parte, quæ postrema est cellula ad septentionem, Sāctissimo ac Beatissimo Ioseph, Virginis Spōso, tamquam eius secretissimo, ac castissimo Custodi, meritò dedicatum est. Vt sequens processionariū indicat. De fonte Beatissimæ Virginis iuxta Ciuitatē Nazareth, & de Ecclesia sub eius nomine ibi constructa. Item de lapide super quem sedebat Iesus cū discipulis suis, quādo illuc, illis diuertere contingebat. Et de loco vbi eum præcipitare voluerunt Nazareni, de his in quā nostra non fuit intentio pertractare. Hæc autem quæ rudi ac simplici stylo digessimus ad summi Dei gloriam, Immaculatę Virginis memoriam, Sanctæ fidei propagationem, & piorum fidelium deuotionem, sincera, ac pura fide, vt præsentes vidimus, & audiuimus, enarrare, testari, futurorumque memoriæ tradere, curauimus.

PROCESSIO:

Ad Altare Sanctissimæ Dei Genitricis Annunciatæ.

LITANIAE S. DOMVS NAZARETH, quæ hodie Lauretana dicitur.

Kyrie eleison. Christe eleison. Kyrie eleison. Christe audi nos. Christe exaudi nos.

Pater

86. Page from the 1628 booklet. It is the first page of the "Processional" prepared by Fr. Tommaso Obiscini da Navaro for the Shrine of Nazareth.

of celebrating the Votive Mass of the Annunciation often during the year.

Assistance to pilgrims

A Shrine presupposes a "presence" of pilgrims. Up until the middle of this century, due to times, difficulties in travelling and other problems, a large number of pilgrims did not appear in

87. The Casa Nova or New Hostel of pilgrims

the Holy Land. But nevertheless, whether there are few or many pilgrims, we must provide adequate lodging for them. And so, since the early years of their stay the Franciscans at Nazareth were concerned about accomodating the basic needs of their pilgrims here in a land which just did not have the things which simple foresight would provide — not only then, but also until not a few years back. The chronicler Verniero could write around the year 1635 that "this Holy House (was) much used by devout pilgrims of diverse nations because of the fine accommodations of a hotel (that is lodging) which they now find there".

Pilgrims, for almost two centuries usually were accomodated in the convent itself, in a section purposely reserved for them. About this particular activity as about the Friar "Guide" there are many examples particularly in the "diaries" of these pilgrims or even non catholic travellers. During the third decade of the last century there existed a hospice for pilgrims which was separate from the convent. Even though it was enlarged and improved down through the ages it has always been inadequate. In 1897 it was replaced by a new large building. The present Casa-Nova was completely remodeled and made more efficient in 1964.

It would not be out of place to draw up a list, even though succinctly, of the personalities guested by the Franciscans of Nazareth. Here it will be sufficient to name Napoleon Bonapart with his Major General in April 1799 after the battle of Tabor (also called of Nazareth), and the famous writer A. De Lamartine who came in 1832. While the Casa Nova was honored in 1902 by the stay of blessed Luigi Guanella, four years later its guest was the then Bishop Angelo Roncalli. We can end these references by mentioning the short stop in the convent made by the Holy Father Paul VI on January 5, 1964.

Nota —
Molti altri soldati
morirono, e furono
sepolti nel comune
Cimiterio de' quali
io ne so' il nome, ne
il numero, perchè non
mi incomodavano facendo
tutto da sè sine
cruce, luce, et sine
aqua benedicta

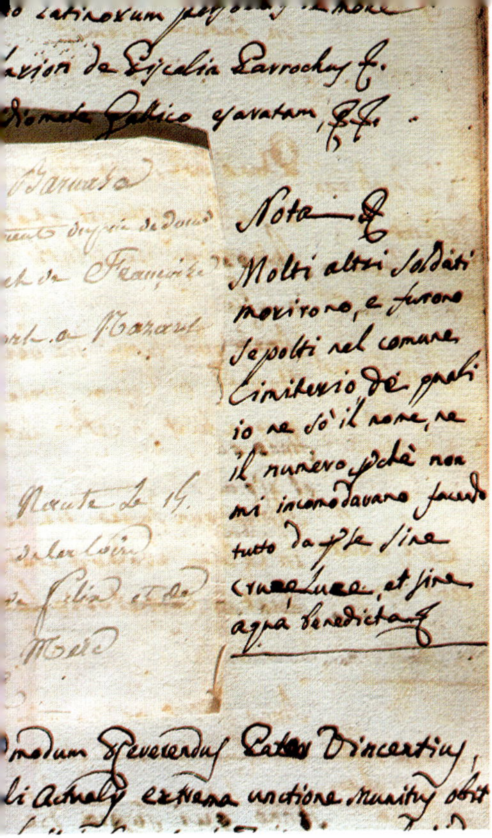

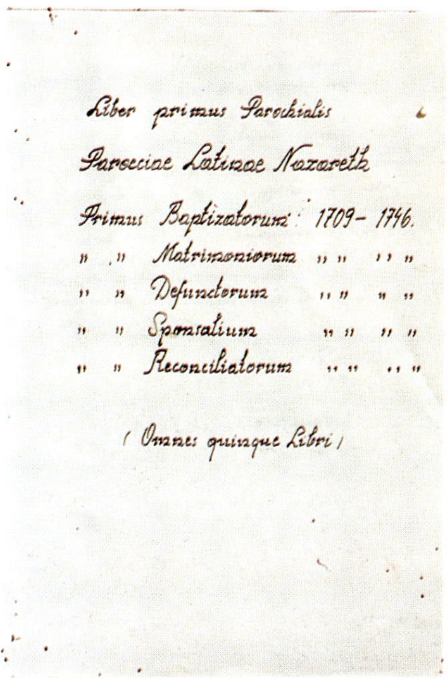

Liber primus Parochialis
Paroeciae Latinae Nazareth
Primus Baptizatorum: 1709 - 1746.
" " Matrimoniorum " " " "
" " Defunctorum " " " "
" " Sponsalium " " " "
" " Reconciliatorum " " " "
(Omnes quinque Libri)

88. Lists of the parish register at Nazareth from 1709 to 1740.

Rebirth of Catholic Life: the Latin Parish

Little is known in a precise fashion about the origins of the Latin Parish of Nazareth, since the older parish registers and related documents became lost in the sudden sack of the convent in 1708. From the reports of the Fathers Custos to the Sacred Congregation of the Propagation of the Faith it seems that a little after the middle of the 1600's there was a core of Catholics of a variety of origins who clustered around the Convent as its clientele or under its protection. The difficult — not to say impossible — living conditions in which the religious found themselves in general, especially during the first century of their stay in Nazareth, had been a determining factor in any normal development of a Catholic Community. Only during the 1700's could it be considered a worthwhile entity both in regard to numbers (more than 800 persons) and in regard to organized Christian life, with a Franciscan Third Order and other pious associations. A "prospectus" of souls from 1664 to 1848, which is useful to have a general idea of the development of the parish just on the basis of numbers, has been compiled by P. Lemmens using figures from various documents.

When conditions in the surrounding area and the general political climate improved, both the parish of Nazareth felt the benefits, and then Catholicism was ready to spread into many parts of

THE PARISH OF NAZARETH FROM 1620 TO 1993

Year	Parishioners
1620	1
1691	24
1715	85
1734	150
1755	344
1832	579
1856	698
1900	1335
1950	2017
1970	3650
1974	4090
1987	4870
1993	5000

Galilee. And actually, especially after the middle of the last century, through the assistance of the Franciscans of Nazareth, new parishes began to be established as well as organized Catholic Communities such as Jaffo (administered today by the Latin Patriarchate), Migdal (today destroyed along with the village), Cana of Galilee, Reine (administered today by the Latin Patriarchate),

89. The computer room of Terra Santa College of Nazareth.

Tiberias (today reviving with some parishioners), Safed (the Catholic Community suddenly disappeared because its members left), etc.

On the right a detail of a "note" of the pastor about a certain soldier of Napoleon:

Keep in mind that the Franciscan pastor in Nazareth has the "cura animarum" of other Catholic rites also. This applies when their own pastors are absent, even temporarily. the Sacred Congregation of the Propagation of Faith determined this in 1780.

Academic Activity

In 1628 the Sacred Congregation of the Propagation of the Faith directed Fr. Custos of the Holy Land "to facilitate communication between those countries (which refers to the Near East in general) and Rome, it would be good that some Friars of mature age be charged with teaching the Latin language to youth of those cities where they were". In 1632 that Sacred Congregation again spoke of the matter: "May your Paternity keep in mind the conservation and augmentation of schools to teach everyone the Latin language...". In their turn the **Statuta pro Terra Sancta** resulting from the General Chapter of Toledo in 1645 offer more precise directives on the matter: at Jerusalem, at Bethlehem and at Nazareth let there be given scholastic instructions to the boys of the parish up to the age of nine years, and let them be given a meal at noon, and when evening comes let them be sent to their homes. All this is the picture from indirect reports. But they do make it clear that there has been a steady, continual development so that we can truthfully say that there in Nazareth, even during those early decades after 1620 there was a small parochial school even though it was most rudimentary. And we presume that it too experienced vicissitudes similar to those inflicted on the convent and the Friars themselves.

After searching the documents, Fr. Lemmens was able to highlight some statistics of the academic "progress" in the parochial school of Nazareth from 1696 to 1848. In the second half of the last century a French magazine from Paris could state that "ordinary instructions were quite widespread among the Catholics of Palestine and especially among the Catholics of the Latin Rite (with the exception of recent conversions) there were no unlettered people and this was due to the schools of the Franciscan Fathers. In their schools besides the customary elementary material in the Arabic language, also the French and Italian languages were taught.

Relations with Christians of the Oriental Rites.

Too little is known about the actual numerical and rite-affiliation composition of the population of Nazareth during the 17th and 18th centuries to make a study which could claim to be recognized as valid historically. Furthermore, although the normal term "oriental christians" is convenient for making oneself understood, in practice many distinctions must be made among Catholics and Orthodox, as well as other distinctions among the respective rites. In the case of Nazareth, again, since we are dealing with such a poor and small village lasting as such down to the dawn of this century, with a usually unstable population, the normal activities involved themselves in the little interests

90. The outside of the "Synagogue" now the Greek Catholic church of Nazareth.

and relations typical of peasants. Therefore we are limiting ourselves to some data of a more widespread nature which then adjusted themselves to the local customs, color and surroundings. It is useless to go back to the 1600's since documents are so scarce from that period. We have an interesting observation in 1730 at the time of the construction of the new church, when some "schismatic heretics" were around who tried to stop the work, and then at the time of the solemn blessing we find "heretics and Turks" participating in great numbers. In 1741 a significant group of Greek Orthodox of Nazareth with one of their priests decided to become Catholic and to do this they came to Fr. Bruno da Solerio, Guardian of the convent and also the civil chief of the countryside. The solution lasting until today, gave rise to a whole series of complications and difficulties with severe harm also to the Friars. Nevertheless the whole project did find a happy solution. The Friars not only did not force the new Catholics to become Latins, but allowed them to keep their rite and also gave over to them, as a place for their service, the so-called "Synagogue of Christ". This situation could be considered as the beginning of the Greek parish of Nazareth. But its existence was not an easy one and it experienced many crosses and changes before it came into its own.

A glimpse of the Nazareth situation as it was in 1764 shows up in the relations between the Custos Fr. Paolo da Piacenza and the Sacred Congregation of the Propagation of Faith. At that time, apart from the Shrine of the Annunciation there was no other church that normally was being serviced. Nor were there other priests than the Friars. And it follows that: "The exact number of Catholics of Nazareth cannot be given, since at the present time it has become a land of refuge. Now suddenly there are four families coming to live there; and tomorrow six are leaving". And among the Catholics he explains that "they are almost all Orientals, and except for a few Syrians, Copts, Chaldeans, Maronites and Greeks they are almost all Latins "ab immemorabili". Although those of other rites received the sacraments from the Latin clergy, so also in other matters they were living in the spirit of the encyclical of His Holiness Benedict XIV".

There was a special event in 1837 when "a good number of Schismatic Greeks, desiring to be taken into the bossom of the Catholic Church, made the condition that they pass over from the Greek to the Latin rite. The matter was discussed by the Sacred Congregation of the Propagation of the Faith and then presented to the Supreme Pontiff and he received the request favorably.

Evidently these attitudes even in themselves express a decision against the Franciscans. They, for their part in order to remain very practical, particularly in the area of giving assistance, sought to be generous to anyone in need without distinction of type, and that became known by pilgrims and travellers as is seen from their "journals". And, as a characteristic of the present time let us note that among the consecrating Bishops of the altars of the new basilica of Nazareth we find a Greek Catholic bishop and a Maronite bishop. And in closing keep in mind the solemn ecumenical meeting with the religious leaders of the non Catholic community, Abyssinians, Armenians, Copts, Greeks and Protestants which took place March 26, 1969 in that same basilica, on the occasion of the celebration of its consecration.

91. Cana of Galilea

92. Cana of Galilee. The chapel of St. Bartholomew.

This Franciscan pilgrims activity over the span of many centuries was the forerunner of the modern pilgrimage. Little by little, always with that same Christian spirit, with patience and their typical steadfastness they reconsecrated the area with churches and chapels and so, here and there, restored centers of Catholic life.

93. Nazareth. Chapel of the Mensa Christi.

94. Chapel of Mount Tabor.

95. The Church of St. Peter in Tiberias.

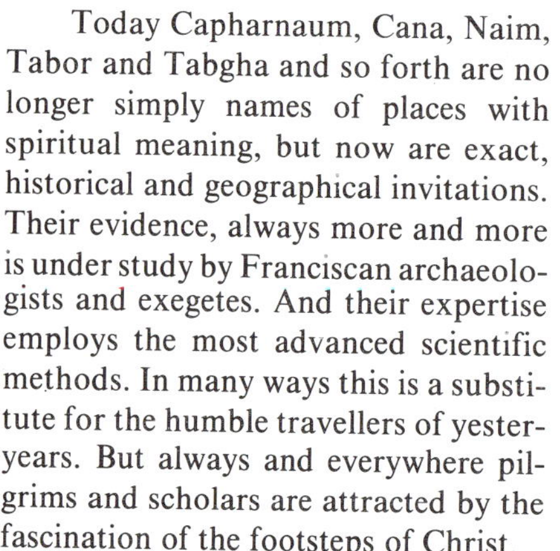

Today Capharnaum, Cana, Naim, Tabor and Tabgha and so forth are no longer simply names of places with spiritual meaning, but now are exact, historical and geographical invitations. Their evidence, always more and more is under study by Franciscan archaeologists and exegetes. And their expertise employs the most advanced scientific methods. In many ways this is a substitute for the humble travellers of yesteryears. But always and everywhere pilgrims and scholars are attracted by the fascination of the footsteps of Christ.

96. The ruins of Capharnaum.

INDEX

COLLABORATORS:

Texts:	Alliata P. Eugenio Brlek P. Metodio Piccirillo P. Michele Pirone Prof. Bartolomeo
English Translation and Editor	Musholt P. Silas
Photographs	Garo Nalbandian Piccirillo P. Michele Vuk P. Tomaslav
Pagination	Adriana and Marino Ferrari

4201-XI-1995